Sidney C. Walker

How to Get More Comfortable ASKING FOR REFERRALS

A SPECIAL REPORT

Published by High Plains Publications
Longmont, Colorado

Formatting Supervision by Tom Raddemann
Cover Design by Robert L. Schram

10 9 8 7 6 5 4 3 2 1

Printed in the United States of America.

ISBN 0-9621177-3-0

Thank You

There are always a lot of people involved in a project of this nature. I would like to thank everyone listed below for their recent contributions to this special report. I would also like to acknowledge my many clients for their input and ideas over the years. Thanks to you all.

G. P. Chokru, Bart Daniel, Lon Davidson, John Devine,
Herb Gallop, Clint Gibson, Rich Greenawalt, Mike Harp,
Mark Janci, Phil Kline, Jerry Kramer, Lori Kranz,
Gerry Maurer, Amy Noel, Mike Parker, Julie Prince,
Tom Raddemann, Scott Richards, Rusty Sandberg,
Bob Schram, Mike Sebesta, Gary Simpson,
Don Skadow, Lee Slavutin, Rick Stuller,
Russ Thompson, Barbara Treadwell,
Paul Twedt, David Whitaker,
Pat Whitaker, Howard Wight,
Charles Wigington,
& Brig Young.

Special thanks to my wife Linda and our daughter Tian for their support and generosity in giving me time to complete this project.

Author's Note

Getting the right information in the shortest amount of time is more important than ever. This special report is to the point. It could be considered a summary of my research on *asking for referrals*. I recommend that you take the time required to give this material your full attention. It won't take long to read, and I promise the time will be well invested. You will either get insights that are critical to your business success or you will get validation for what you are doing or want to do.

I have purposely limited the highlighting of text to occasional italics so you can decide for yourself what is important to you as you read. I have included a summary of key points at the end for a quick review.

Asking for referrals is more complicated than it looks. Yet it is a skill that can be mastered with modest risk and effort on your part. I wish you the greatest success in this endeavor.

SID WALKER

Longmont, Colorado

Contents

PART ONE

Benefits, Purpose, and Definitions

IMAGINE THIS ...

Imagine this: The telephone rings and the person on the other end of the line says, "I was talking to my friend Tom Johnson the other day and he had great things to say about you and the work you did for him. I would like to meet you and see if you might be able to help me in some of the same ways you helped Tom."

How would a call like that make you feel?

Imagine this: You are with a client who has just bought your service and you ask her, "Would you be willing to introduce me to people you know so I could show them the kind of work I do?" And she says, "Sure, I would be happy to! I can think of several people you should meet."

How would a response like that make you feel?

Besides feeling good about the fact that people like you and trust you enough to give you referrals or introductions to people they know, there are many other powerful benefits for getting referred leads. Numerous studies, formal and informal, have been done on the effectiveness of getting referred leads with similar conclusions. Here are some *typical findings*:

- You will get to see two to three times more people when you are referred in.

- The people you are referred to will establish rapport and trust with you more quickly because of the mutual acquaintance.

- The people you are referred to will be more open to listening to you and giving your offer serious consideration.

- Prospects you have been referred to are two to three times more likely to buy.

- Prospects you have been referred to are more likely to *give you* referrals at the end of the sales process.

- You don't have to make as many cold calls, maybe none.

- You don't have to spend a fortune on less effective means of identifying prospects.

The bottom line: If the people you call on are two to three times more likely to see you and two to three times more likely to buy, what is that going to do to your income? I am sure you will agree that the potential benefits that come from being referred to new business are substantial.

THE PURPOSE OF THIS SPECIAL REPORT

My purpose in writing this special report is to *share proven methods for making it more comfortable to consistently ask for and get quality referrals to new business.* This material is *not* meant to be a restatement of the conventional wisdom about asking for referrals. My research shows that most sales-people experience some resistance to asking for referrals even if they *know* what to do and say. This material is about how to overcome that resistance. It's about how to overcome the most common psychological barriers to asking for referrals. *It's for the people who know they can and should be asking for referrals to new business, but are not.* This material is designed to get you folks to take action. The time you spend asking for and getting referrals to new business, for most sales-people, is one of the most highly profitable activities you can do.

THE DEFINITION OF A REFERRAL

Let's take a moment to get more clearly aligned on our definition of the phrase "getting referrals." When you get a referral, you typically have been given the name of another person by someone you have established some kind of a relationship with. The relationship could be very brief, as in simply spending a few minutes with someone socially or the result of a sales call where you met someone for a few minutes to tell them about the kind of work you do. Or, the relationship with the person giving you names could be much more involved, as with that of friend, acquaintance, client, or customer.

Generally speaking, the stronger the relationship between the referror (the person giving you names) and the referral (the person they are referring you to), the more powerful the referral. The phrase "power referral" has been used to describe a referral that comes from someone who has a substantial influence with the person they are referring. This could be a relative or close friend. Or, in the case of a work-related relationship, it could be someone's manager or partner doing the referring. A New York Life study concluded that when the referror had significant influence with the person they were referring, it was twice as effective as a referral from a social acquaintance. Twice as effective, in this case, meant that twice as many people bought something when the introduction was the result of a power referral.

A referral can be an endorsement by your client of you and your service, or simply a social introduction. In doing many years of peak performance coaching work with life insurance agents, I usually encourage them to keep the process of getting referrals more social rather than an endorsement of their product or service. It is much easier to get names from your clients if you are simply asking to be introduced to other people. Otherwise, asking for an endorsement of your product or service tends to make your clients think in terms of who they know that needs what they just bought. In some cases, this is exactly what you want them to be thinking. However, when the product is life insurance, this gives your clients the difficult task of deciding who they know that needs life insurance. Most people would have a difficult time with that question because in our society, we know very little about other people's financial situations. The agent will have much greater success asking his clients who they know who is doing well financially or who just got a big promotion. Now the agent can take the more social approach of simply wanting to be introduced to someone who is doing well to see if they could be a potential resource to that person.

There are situations where referrals are of very little help, such as when you are looking for prospects that fit very specific qualifications. For example, I have a client who only works with people who have been recently turned down for large amounts of life insurance. It is unlikely that any of his clients or friends are going to know who has recently been turned down for large amounts of life insurance. Most people don't share that kind of information even if they know of someone in that situation.

There are situations where people feel it is *inappropriate* to give referrals. For example, you are a life insurance agent doing some planning with a partner in a large CPA firm. The partner's firm has two life insurance companies as clients. When you ask the partner to give you referrals, his response is that he would be uncomfortable endorsing one company over the other. He explains that showing favoritism could lead to complications that he would rather avoid. So there are situations where referrals either don't work very well or are not appropriate. For the most part, referrals are the most potent source of new business for most salespeople most of the time.

WHY DO REFERRALS WORK SO WELL?

Why do referrals work so well in terms of leading to more sales than with any other kind of lead? First of all, you have a much greater chance of getting in to see a referred lead as opposed to a cold call. Most people will give you a few minutes of their time, regardless of whether or not they are interested in what you have to offer, simply out of respect for their friend who referred you. They figure you would not have been referred if you didn't have something to offer that was of value.

Furthermore, we generally like to do business with people that we know and trust. When you are introduced or referred, you immediately start off with the benefit of having a mutual acquaintance. Having things in common is the basis of rapport, and rapport has become a basic requirement for making a sale today. When was the last time you made a sale if the rapport wasn't there?

Being referred or being introduced creates a feeling of familiarity. Loosely interpreted, the word "familiarity" comes from the word "family." If you are considered "family" or "one of the group," you have a lot in common. The more you have in common with someone else, the stronger the initial rapport. The stronger the initial rapport, the more likely something positive will develop from the relationship. So when you're referred or introduced to another person by their friend, you are assumed to be like them in some way. There is almost an expectation that you are going to get along because of having the friend in common. Of course, being referred or introduced does not guarantee that a positive relationship will develop. However, with a referral or introduction, the likelihood of being received on a favorable basis is extremely high.

PART TWO
Challenges and Solutions

SOME WILL AND SOME WON'T

What are the criteria you would use to determine if you were going to give someone referrals to people you know? Let's assume for a moment that you have worked with Frank, the financial advisor, and that you liked the work he did. Would you offer the names of your friends right there on the spot, unsolicited? Probably not, but a possibility. You don't know if Frank even wants names. It might not even occur to you to offer names unless you had some knowledge of the sales process. You may feel that your friends have their own advisors they are happy with, and that you don't want to involve yourself in such a personal way. If you did suspect that Frank would like some names, wouldn't you feel better about Frank's confidence level if he asked you for them? And even if Frank did ask you for names, would you have to consider how you would look to your friends by referring Frank? Would people think more or less of you for referring Frank? How would Frank feel about you if you gave him names of people that didn't result in any business? Would that bother you? Would it bother you enough to not want to give any referrals? You can see that being asked to give introductions to your friends can easily become very psychologically complex.

There has been a lot of study and documentation of what is called *social styles*. These are general behavior preferences that can be readily observed in humans. Two basic continuums determine social style. One continuum has *assertive* on one side and *more cautious* on the other. The other continuum has *thinking* on one side and *feeling* on the other. When you lay these two continuums one on top of the other to form four right-angle quadrants, it creates four basic social styles. The four groups are: *assertive thinkers*, *assertive feelers*, *more cautious thinkers,* and *more cautious feelers*.

Generally speaking, the *assertive* feelers and thinkers are going to be more comfortable giving you referrals. They like to have influence over other people and they like to test that influence. On the other hand, the *more cautious* thinkers and feelers are not as interested in testing their influence. They want to get along and be liked at all costs, and are much less likely to want to risk any potential conflicts by making introductions or giving referrals.

When you look at the makeup of the population, roughly speaking, the *assertive thinkers* make up about 20% of the population, the *assertive feelers* about 10%. So about 30% of the population are generally open to giving referrals if they like you and what you are doing. The *more cautious feelers* are the largest group at 50%, and the *more cautious thinkers* are 20%. Therefore, about 70% of the population are not very excited about making introductions.

There is an additional positive factor in favor of getting referrals. As human beings, we are much more complicated than any four-quadrant profile can predict. In fact, most social style profiles break the four main quadrants down into 16 additional identifiable profiles. What this means is that there is a large group of the *more cautious thinkers* and *more cautious feelers* who have a backup social style that is more assertive. My guess is that about one-third to one-half of the *more cautious* group has a backup style that is assertive and they are, therefore, generally open to giving referrals under the right conditions.

What does all this mean in terms of who is comfortable giving referrals? Generally speaking, in terms of social styles, I predict that approximately 50% of any mixed group of people are going to be comfortable giving referrals if they like you and what you are offering. This, of course, means that the other 50% of the group are not going to be comfortable introducing you to anyone. So if you are expecting that everyone will give you referrals, you are going to be very disappointed.

The reality is that there is a large group of people who are never going to be comfortable giving you referrals no matter what you do. To feel you have failed in some way when you don't get referrals is an inappropriate response to the situation. Unfortunately, many salespeople feel they have failed when they don't get referrals. Salespeople are typically taught by the sales culture that they should expect or demand referrals from everyone they meet or sell products to. Then, when they don't get them, the logical conclusion is to feel like they have failed or didn't do the process correctly. If you are told that you should be getting referrals from everyone and you don't get them several times in a row, what often happens is you stop asking. The conflict is too great. It is easier not to deal with it. It is easier not to ask.

There is a famous quote that is credited to W. C. Bennett which says: *"Blessed is he who expects no gratitude, for he shall not be disappointed."* Applied to our subject of asking for referrals, this roughly translates to: Rather than be disappointed, change your expectation. If half of the people you establish some kind of relationship with give you referrals, you are at the head of the class.

IT'S MORE COMPLICATED THAN IT LOOKS

If getting referrals works so well, why isn't everybody doing it? You would think that most salespeople would see the logic and power of asking for referred leads and be asking every chance they get. Yet this is not the case at all. The majority of salespeople have difficulty in asking for referrals or have had some resistance to asking for referrals in the past. In my decade and a half as a peak performance coach, primarily to financial services salespeople, I have been regularly surprised and amazed at the number of salespeople who do not ask for referrals. They don't ask when they know it's the best way for them to obtain new business. Some salespeople have so much resistance to asking for referrals they have told me they would rather make cold calls than ask for referrals!

Where does this discomfort with the referral process come from? The answer is much more complex than you might think. As we discussed, the process of giving referrals is complex for the person being asked to give them. *Asking* for referrals is even more psychologically complicated. This might surprise you because the process looks so simple and it is often presented that way in training. You might be told that all you have to do is ask for referrals. True enough, all we have to do is ask, but let's look at what can keep a salesperson from asking.

There are numerous topics to consider. I will list them first to give you an overview and then discuss each of the conflicts and how they can be resolved.

Mechanically Based Conflicts

- Some people simply forget to ask.

- Some people don't leave enough time to ask when they are with people.

Rejection-based Conflicts

- Some people are afraid of how they will feel if their client doesn't give them any referrals.

- Some people are afraid of what others will think of them if they ask for their help.
    - Some are afraid they will look less than successful if

they ask for referrals.
- Some feel asking for referrals is unprofessional.
- Some say that asking for referrals makes them feel like they are begging.

• Some people have had a few bad experiences and decided it wasn't worth the effort.

Approach-based Conflicts

• Some people are not comfortable with what to say.

• Some people feel that they don't deserve referrals.

• Some people are afraid of making other people uncomfortable.

MECHANICALLY BASED CONFLICTS

The first group of topics falls under the heading of what I call *mechanical* conflicts. This type of conflict is the easiest to remedy since it is usually only a matter of adjusting your priorities. For example, if you have no psychological barriers to asking for referrals and you are just forgetting to ask, you simply make asking for referrals a priority. You do this by creating obvious notes on your paperwork or your daytimer that will remind you to ask for referrals. You can put a sticker on your watch that indicates "ask," or "ref." If a client asks you what the dot is on your watch, you can say it is to remind you to ask a couple of key questions. The perfect situation is when your client or prospect asks you what the dot is on your watch and the timing is right to ask for referrals. The key is to put reminders in a place where you will have to look before you leave an appointment.

Some people say they like to get referrals after someone buys, but they often run out of time. This *is* a challenge. There is often a lot of paperwork and many details to be taken care of at the time of a sale. However, you have to consider the value of referred leads in your business. If they have proven to be highly profitable, then asking for referrals is probably one of the most important things you can do after you've made a sale. *Make it a priority!* If something doesn't get done, make it something other than asking for referrals. Again, we're assuming that you have no resistance to asking for referrals, that it's simply a matter of making it important enough to ask.

There are other ways to give yourself more time to ask for referrals. You can shorten another part of your presentation so you have more time to ask for referrals. You can make the amount of time you allocate for your referral presentation longer. Or you can schedule another time to get back with people for any number of reasons and then include asking for referrals. If your sales process requires two or more meetings, it's easy to ask for referrals at one of the follow-up meetings. If you are doing a one-call presentation and close, your options are more limited. Whatever you do, make it a priority and ask!

The bottom line is this: If you have no psychological resistance to asking for referrals and you are not asking, *it is not a priority*. Remember, we all have the same amount of time in a workday. One of the big reasons some people sell so much more than others is that they make getting referrals as important as making the sale. With the substantial likelihood that a referred lead will turn into a sale, you can't afford not to ask.

REJECTION-BASED CONFLICTS

The rejection-based conflicts are more difficult to resolve. These include *being afraid of how you will feel if your client doesn't give you any referrals* and *being afraid of what others will think of you if you ask for their help*. Some people are *afraid they will look less than successful or professional* if they ask for referrals. Some people say they *feel like they are begging* when they ask for referrals. Then there is the common situation of asking for referrals, *having a few negative experiences, and then deciding it isn't worth the effort*. In all these situations, there is a fear of rejection that must be neutralized before the salesperson is ever going to be comfortable enough to ask for referrals.

What do you do if you are afraid of what others will think if you ask them for help? Some salespeople have told me that they feel less than professional or that they feel like they are begging if they ask for referrals. Or they are concerned that their new client will think they are less than successful or professional if they need to ask for introductions.

The kind of business you are in is an important factor. For many years it has been considered unprofessional and even unethical to ask for referrals in many professions like those of doctors, dentists, accountants, and attorneys, to name a few. This thinking has tended to make some people think that if you are really professional, people will come to you.

There is a difference between being in a business where you have something that people *have* to come to you for, such as medicine. If you are sick or injured, you are going to be motivated to find the right doctor or group of people who can deal with your problem. But what if your problem is not so urgent, such as with life insurance or investments? You know you need to do some planning for your financial future, but you don't have to do it today. If you're bleeding, you need medical attention right now! If you need to plan your financial future, you have much more time to decide what to do. This discretionary time factor is what changes how we market our products and services. Here is a key question to ponder: Because the need to address a particular problem is less urgent, does that make the people who provide this service less professional? The answer is, of course not!

Does the fact that you have to get people to stop and deal with a problem they could have in the future make you less professional? Of course not. Some form of selling and self-promotion is required of everyone who presents solutions to future problems. Getting people to take the time to become aware of problems they now face or will face, educating them on the options for solving their problems, and then helping them make an informed decision, is as professional as you can get. Not to get information on potential future problems is generally considered irresponsible behavior. The one factor we have to include here is that each person gets to decide if she wants to deal with the particular future problem you are addressing. She may decide to take the time now or may defer to another time. Again, whether people are ready to deal with the problems and solutions you are presenting has very little to do with whether you are a professional at what you do. This is an extremely important distinction to make.

So unless you are in a profession that requires people to take immediate action, you are going to have to do some self-promotion. You are going to have to ask people if they are ready to talk about what you have to offer. If you are talking to people you have been introduced to by other satisfied customers, you are going to be many times more effective. It's the difference between saying to people, "Hi, would you like to buy some life insurance today?" and "I was talking to a friend of yours recently who is excited about the service we are offering and mentioned to me that you might also have an interest in what we are doing." Which approach do you think is going to be more successful? Which approach sounds easier and more self-fulfilling for the salesperson?

The reality is that unless you are in a profession where the need is either very obvious or very immediate, you are going to have to get people's interest and attention about what life could be like in the future with your product or service.

In my own case, I consider myself a professional at what I do. And still, no matter how many clients someone thinks I have, or how successful someone thinks I am, I like to have people promoting me and my work as long as they believe in me. I know that my profession deals with changes people can make in their lives at some point in the future. I know that people will survive without knowing who I am and what I can do for them. I also know that there will be a lot of people who will be better off because I was a part of their lives. As much as possible, I want to be a contributing factor in other people's lives. If they buy something from me, that's wonderful, but not a requirement.

If you take a professional approach to your work, you *are* a professional. Asking for referrals is simply part of being a professional for many salespeople. If someone else thinks you are less than professional because you are asking for their help, that's their issue, and not really your problem. Not only is it their issue, there is no certainty that what they are saying is even the *real* issue. People will often complain about one problem when what is actually bothering them is something very different. People, in general, are incredibly complicated. So unless you want to moonlight as a psychologist and ask your clients if they have an interest in dealing with their unre-solved issues, it is a waste of time to give another thought to their opinions of how you do business. You simply put them in the category of people who are not comfortable giving you referrals. After reading this material, you will know more about the psychology behind asking for referrals than most of your clients are going to know in their lifetime. If they don't want to help you, let it go. A friend of mine once described the futility of trying to teach people things they are not ready to hear: It as if you were a butterfly trying to explain to a larva what it will be like to be a butterfly. The larva would be convinced you had lost your mind.

Feel Like You Are Begging?

Some people tell me they don't like asking their clients "for their help" because it feels like begging. In addition to understanding that many professions require some self-promotion as previously stated, there are other ways to lessen and even eliminate the feeling that you're begging. Much of the material presented in this special report is devoted to changing your perspective and your referror's perspective on asking for referrals to a more positive one. So keep reading and you will get lots of information on how to shift your perspective away from feeling like you are begging. In general, you have to see yourself as a professional who is offering a service or a valuable process that you take people through. If your referror views you as a salesperson asking to use the referror's influence to get you in to see if you can sell his friends something, this *should* feel like begging. However, if both you and your referror see you as a valued advisor who treats people with honor and respect and helps people get what *they* really want, the referror should feel that he is doing his friends a favor by introducing you.

Call Reluctance Is a Logical Response

The fear of rejection is actually a very logical response given the circumstances in a selling situation. Most of us champion an analytical approach to problem solving, especially in business. This is the approach we were originally taught in school. An analytical approach means that there is a presumed correct answer or correct way of doing something that will produce the expected or desired result. This is true when you are adding a column of numbers. There *is* a correct answer. But what makes the analytical approach viable are defined parameters where the values of things remain constant. When you add a column of numbers, the values of the numbers don't change as you add them up. They remain constant. You know for certain what the value of each number is. These exact and stable definitions are not available when you are working with people.

When you are working with people, you are dealing with the human mind, which has an infinite capacity for change and misinterpretation. Can you imagine trying to add a column of numbers that could change in value without telling you or could withhold their values and make you guess what they are? It is not very likely that you would be successful with such a moving target. Yet this is the reality of working with people. It reminds me of the Pepsi television commercial showing the future of basketball. Shaquille O'Neal is going up to the basket for a slam dunk, and at the last second before the ball goes into the basket, the basket moves, causing him to miss an easy shot.

Most of us tend to default to an analytical approach to problem solving because it is what we learned in school; it is logical. The problem is that the analytical approach is too limited to actually work when dealing with the infinite variables that come into play when interacting with people. Not only does the analytical approach not work in dealing with people because of its limitations, it is actually disrespectful. People should not be treated like a column of numbers that you can add up. We are incredibly complicated beings with many defined and undefined feelings, emotions, intentions, desires, hopes, fears, and expectations — all of which have the potential to change at any moment. I call that a moving target.

So based on the way we have been trained, a logical result is to develop call reluctance. Part of our brain thinks we are in control, part of our brain knows we are not in control. This sort of thinking can create some hesitation. When we take an analytical approach in dealing with people, we expect that if we do everything exactly right, we will achieve our objective. What we eventually are forced to find out in sales is that you can do everything perfectly and people can still say no. This causes some big problems. The approach to problem-solving we have been using on a regular basis for most of our lives doesn't work like it used to. Unfortunately, at this point most people make the wrong conclusion. They think there must be something wrong with them, which is usually not the case at all.

The good news is that the problem lies with the approach we are taking to solve the problem, not with the person. We are simply using the wrong approach or the wrong equipment to deal with the problem. I often tell my clients that using an analytical approach when dealing with your own self-promotional issues is the equivalent of trying to play football wearing hockey equipment, including ice skates. You can do it, but it isn't going to be a pleasant experience. You are going to get beatup. This is exactly how most people feel who have any amount of call reluctance.

Shift to a Bigger Perspective

What is required to effectively deal with call reluctance is a shift in your perspective away from the narrow and highly defined focus of the analytical approach. As long as you are working with the perspective that says there is a correct way to ask for referrals and if you do it just right it will work every time, you are in big trouble. It won't be long before you stop asking. The perspective that's required to effectively deal with all the variables involved in dealing with people is the total opposite of the narrow perspective of the analytical. It is as big a perspective as you can get. The shift is to a much broader perspective which better fits the reality I like to call the *prospecting mentality* (the title of my tape program on how to get in the mood to prospect).

The essence of the prospecting mentality is that you don't have any attachment to whether people give you referrals or not. You ask in a way that feels right to you. Then you trust and honor whatever people do. Some people are going to be comfortable helping you and some are not. You don't know who they are going to be and *it doesn't matter who helps you and who doesn't.* You trust that there are plenty of people who will introduce you to people they know. If someone isn't comfortable giving you names, you move on and don't give it another thought. You recognize that some people will never be comfortable introducing you to people they know no matter what you do. In other words, it isn't about whether they like you or not, or believe in what you are doing. They just don't introduce salespeople to the people they know.

The prospecting mentality takes some time to integrate, especially if you are used to thinking only in terms of trying to do everything just right so you get the "right answer" from people. The prospecting mentality as we have defined it may seem very loose. It is! The initial reaction many people have is that you won't get enough referrals if you don't push people. This is more of a style issue. If you are comfortable pushing people for referrals and it's working for you, there's no need to change. If, however, it doesn't feel right to push people and you are pushing because you think it's the only way to make a living, there is a potential problem. If you are pushing people out of fear, that is a negative context, which is going to have a negative impact in some way. If there is negative energy involved in your referral process, it will show up somewhere. For example, the people will be hard to reach, they won't see you, the chemistry won't be there when you finally meet them, or they won't be the caliber of people you want to meet. What is more likely is that if you are uncomfortable pushing people to get referrals and that is what you think you need to do, you are probably not asking at all, which has obvious negative consequences.

What works well to diffuse some of the old "stuck" thinking is a *warm-up*. Like a professional athlete, we need to loosen up and get ourselves in the right frame of mind before we get onto the playing field of self-promotion. See the section of sample warm-ups on page 95.

For a more in-depth discussion of the concepts presented here, listen to my tape programs entitled *The Prospecting Mentality — How to Get in the Right Frame of Mind to Prospect for New Business* and the recording of two live coaching sessions with individual clients entitled *How to Sell Yourself with Power and Integrity*, and *How to Overcome Prospecting Avoidance and Procrastination*.

APPROACH-BASED CONFLICTS

Another source of potential conflict regarding asking for referrals is what I call *approach-based conflicts*. This kind of conflict can show up as *not being comfortable with what to say* or *being afraid of making people uncomfortable by asking for their help*. Some people will go so far as to say that *they don't feel they deserve referrals*.

To understand where some of these conflicts come from, we need to go back 100 years to the roots of our current sales culture, back to the days of the industrial revolution. These were the days of "Robber Barons," "kings of industry," and the Latin phrase "caveat emptor" — let the buyer beware.

The values of this period can be summed up in two words: *dominance* and *control*.

Many of those values from the industrial revolution have carried forward to today's sales culture. The question we are most often asked as salespeople is "What did you sell today?" rather than "Who did you help today?" What is valued is whether or not you made the sale. How you arrived at making the sale is much less important.

The carryover of the dominance and control values into the realm of asking for referrals sounds like "demand referrals," "expect referrals," and "don't work with anyone who won't give you referrals."

If this conventional approach makes you fidget with discomfort, you are not alone. What I have found in my research is that there are only a handful of people, less than 10% of any sales force, that are comfortable with this kind of approach. What typically happens is that everyone else assumes you have to use dominance and control to make a living. Many people try to move in the direction of dominance and control, usually with little or no success, and end up feeling guilty about being too pushy.

Again, I have good news for you. You don't have to use dominance and control to be incredibly successful in sales. In fact, you can be very low-key. The trend today is away from dominance and control for a number of reasons. One big factor is that the consuming public is fed up with it. They want to be treated with respect and get professional assistance in making informed decisions about products and services. Consumers do not want to be treated as a "buying unit" that needs to be conquered, tricked, cajoled, or finessed into a sale with little or no regard for their interests and concerns.

The other big reason the dominance and control approach is losing favor daily is that it's hard on salespeople. What is empowering to salespeople over the long haul is doing work in a way that fits their most deeply held values. People place a high value on making money. But underneath the seemingly dominant need to make money is a care and concern for other people. No one is naturally comfortable with a dominance and control approach. It is a learned skill or an acquired taste like coffee or alcohol. If we believed that we could make a great living treating people with honor and respect, that is the approach most would chose. If we believed we would be treated with honor and respect as a salesperson taking a more humane approach, that is the approach most would choose. Fear, greed, self-doubt, financial pressure, and other forms of negative thinking make a lot of people take what seems to be the more results-oriented approach of dominance and control. But there is a price, a not so obvious price. When you are motivated by negative thoughts and/or emotions, you are creating a negative vision. When you create a negative vision and give it energy by your belief, you begin to bring into being the very thing you fear will happen. It may not happen exactly as you imagined, but the negativity will manifest somewhere in your life. Usually it will show up as money problems, health problems, and communication problems with those who are closest to you, to name a few of the big ones.

Success in selling has traditionally been defined in terms of how many sales you made or how much money you made. People have not often asked how you feel about the sales approach you are using. Are you honoring people and helping them make the decisions that feel right to them, or are you selling them on what you think they should do with little or no regard for their feelings? What is happening more and more is that salespeople are changing to a sales approach based on a *partnership* with the client. So a new question is being asked when someone goes to the podium to talk about how they became "salesperson of the month." The question is, did you do it with honor and respect for the needs and wants of your client, or are you pushing people into sales for your own reward and recognition? This question may not be asked out loud, but it is on the minds of many salespeople in the audience today.

Much of what motivates the dominance and control approach is fear. The original goal in selling was to make the sale. Helping people make the right buying decision for *them* was not really part of the equation. If that happened, it was a bonus but not a focus. Furthermore, the belief was the client could not be trusted to make the right decision, which was to buy the product. They needed the salesperson's help. Prospects have been seen as unmotivated entities who need to be pressured and pushed to buy for their own good. The belief has been that you need to bring your prospects to an emotional frenzy and get them to see your product as the answer to all their problems. In other words, you can't trust people to make the right decision for themselves. You have to force the sale or you might not be able to make a living.

In relation to asking for referrals, what often happens is that the sales culture teaches us to expect or demand referrals. We feel uncomfortable with this approach. However, until more recently it has been more important that we make a living than that we feel comfortable with our approach. We continue to feel the internal conflict; we have to really push ourselves to ask for referrals. Our clients are less than responsive because they are picking up on our conflict. Then one day we notice that we haven't asked for referrals for three months and wonder why our production is down. On top of all these negative effects, we feel guilty because we don't ask for referrals. We end up feeling inadequate because we couldn't do what seems to be relatively easy for other people with less talent and ability. We then spend tremendous amounts of time and money trying to find something that will indirectly fix the problem, like "a better marketing system," which really doesn't exist for most salespeople. By definition, nothing is going to beat a good referral for the reasons we have previously discussed.

Unfortunately, the dominance and control approach is not going to disappear overnight. It is a very stubborn animal. This is a growing problem in most sales cultures because there are two distinct groups emerging: those operating from a context of partnership with prospects and clients, and those still using dominance and control as the basis for their sales approach. Both approaches work in terms of producing sales. The big difference between the two approaches is that the *partnership approach* is based on putting the clients' interests first and helping clients get what they really want. The *dominance and control approach* is based on putting the salesperson's interests first and doing everything possible to make a sale.

We need to look beyond numbers like "sales volume" and ask some more questions to determine which approach has the most overall merit. Questions like: How much of the business that is written stays on the books? How do the clients feel about their interactions with the salesperson? Do they feel that the salesperson put the clients' interests first? Would they recommend this salesperson to their friends? Is the predominant motivation of the salesperson to increase the quality of his clients' lives by helping them get what they really want? Or is the salesperson a predator making sales primarily for his own gain rationalizing that people will be better off owning his product regardless of what their needs and wants happen to be?

If you ask yourself how you want to be treated in the sales process, you are likely to say that you want the salesperson to respect your opinions, desires, feelings, and values. These aspects are generally not respected in an attitude of dominance and control. That is what people are quietly rebelling against.

Salespeople using the dominance and control approach will find it increasingly difficult to make a living as the general public continues to demand greater respect from salespeople. If I feel a salesperson is trying to move me in a direction that does not take into account my feelings on the subject, I will terminate the interview. I don't want to waste my time with someone who has so little respect for me as a human being. I am not saying that people using the dominance and control approach are bad people. Often it is a matter of the salesperson not knowing any better. Dominance and control are all they have ever been shown. Bringing people to a new level of awareness on what really works for all involved takes time, patience, and forgiveness. Changing the predominant values of a 100-year-old sales cultures is no small task. The best ways to contribute to the end of dominance and control as an accepted approach are: 1) dedicate yourself to finding alternatives to dominance and control in your own sales approach, and 2) don't buy anything from salespeople who use dominance and control tactics.

The Power of Your Core Values

If you want to *rid yourself of the approach-based conflicts* related to asking for referrals, you have to make your approach both to selling and to asking for referrals fit your most deeply-held values.

If you're into dominance and control, there is lots of information out there on how to move people into a corner and twist their arm until they buy. However, I doubt that you are comfortable with the dominance and control approach or you wouldn't be reading this book. The changes you most likely need to make are going to be letting go of anything that feels like dominance and control and shifting to an approach that honors and respects the judgment, desires, feelings, and values of your prospect or client.

I like to say that instead of moving your prospects into a corner, *you help them figure out what is important to them and why it's important.* And you *always leave them a way out.* You don't want the pressure to buy to come from you telling them what they should do. You want the pressure to buy to come from them verbalizing to you what they really want and why they want it. When people verbalize what they want and why, this creates the motivation people need to take action. You are still there as a catalyst and to offer your expertise, but you are *on their side of the table* helping them get what they want, rather than an adversary trying to talk them into something. This is a big transition for many salespeople to make who have not given much thought to an alternative to the dominance and control approach.

You may be in a sales office where the main values of the culture are still based on the dominance and control approach. The best thing to do in this case is to stay focused on what feels intuitively right to you. If you see someone else being successful with an approach that is not comfortable for you, it is tempting. But it won't work for you in the long run. Don't waste your time. Find the approach that fits your values and stick with it. You will learn how to make it work for you and make more sales as a result. Be patient and have some trust and faith. Fortunately, in most sales environments, if you are making an average number of sales for your experience level, you will have some freedom to develop your own style.

What Are Your Core Sales Values?

How do you feel about your approach to selling? What are the predominant values expressed by your interactions with the people you call on?

- Are you excited to get to work in the morning?

- Do you feel empowered by your sales approach and the process you take people through?

- Are your clients empowered by your sales approach and the process you take them through?

- Will your clients be impressed enough with you and your approach to want to refer you to their friends?

- If your answer to any of the above questions is no, what do you need to do differently?

The following lists describe two distinctly different approaches to selling, or two different paradigms. The first is the more traditional, adversarial paradigm based on dominance and control. The second is the newer kid on the block, the approach based on being in "partnership" with your client. As you read through both lists, ask yourself who you would rather work with if *you* were the prospect or client. Then ask yourself, if you were the client being asked for referrals, which type of salesperson would you be most comfortable introducing to your friends? Then ask yourself which values *you* are demonstrating in your sales approach.

Dominance & Control Paradigm

- You see your prospects and clients as something to be conquered.

- You agree with this statement: "Making the sale is the only thing that really counts."

- When it comes to your product or service, you feel that most people need to be told what to do and talked into doing it.

- You see selling as a process you take people through that is designed to get them to buy your product every time.

- What *you* think your client should do is the predominant theme of your closing presentation.

- If you don't make the sale, you have failed.

Partnership Paradigm

- You honor your clients as people just like yourself with unique needs, wants and desires who want solutions to their problems that are the most appropriate for their needs and budget.

- Your main objective is to help people make an educated decision that feels right to them, which includes not buying anything at this time as a viable option.

- You trust your clients to make the right decision for themselves at the completion of your process.

- You view selling as a process to help your clients get a clear sense of what their specific problem is; show them what the options are to solving that problem, and finally you help them make an informed decision that feels right to them (fits their values).

- What your clients say they want and why they want it (not what *you* think they should do) is the predominant theme of your closing presentation.

- You have succeeded if you have helped your clients make a decision that feels right to them, whether a sale was made or not.

Which type of salesperson would you rather work with?

Which would you feel more comfortable introducing to your friends? Which kind of salesperson is going to make the most money and be the happiest in the long run?

If you feel conflict with any part of the sales process you are taking people through, that conflict is going to show up when you go to ask for referrals. Your clients will subconsciously pick up on your conflict and be much less likely to want to refer you to people they know, even if they bought something from you.

Stop and take an inventory of the parts of your sales process that you are not comfortable with and imagine some alternatives that could work for you. One way to get at some options is to simply ask yourself how *you* would want to be treated. The days of the "slick salesman," the person who can sell ice cubes to Eskimos, are out of step with how consumers want to be treated. The general public is a lot smarter and more sophisticated than ever. Communication all over the world on every subject imaginable is practically instant. Consumers want salespeople who can help them solve problems with solutions that will work and that fit their unique situation. We want to work with informed professional people that will put our interests first. Sound idealistic? It is. It is also very real today.

Advanced technology creates many wonderful things to make our lives easier. But there are drawbacks that are actually to our advantage. The use of computers tends to depersonalize how we do business and lessen the amount of person-to-person contact. More than ever, people want to do business with someone they know. Even better, someone they like and trust. The desire to work with someone who knows your situation is stronger than ever. Trying to get problems resolved with people you have never spoken to before and will likely never speak to again is becoming more and more common. So much so that long-term relationships are becoming the premium.

Be Someone People Want to Refer

Another powerful way to resolve approach-based conflicts is to be the kind of person people want to refer to their friends. Or be the kind of person that other people *want* to help.

The following list contains some of the characteristics of the type of people you *want* to help:

- Possess a positive attitude.
- Are solution-oriented rather than problem-oriented.
- Believe in their product or service.
- Have a friendly sense of humor.
- Find things to compliment people on.
- Operate from a win-win approach.
- Are patient listeners.
- Demonstrate knowledge and sensitivity to the different social styles.
- Have a real desire to help people get what they want.
- Have a sense of purpose and meaningfulness about helping people in general.
- Assist people in defining their dominant motivation (what's important and why).
- Tend not to lead people into corners with no way out.
- Create an open and nonjudgmental atmosphere.

What characteristics would you add to the list?

It's Not What You Say, It's How You Say It

Many salespeople make the mistake of thinking they need the exact right words before they can ask someone for referrals.

They even think that if they can get the exact right words, people will say yes to them all the time. The reality is that the attitude and feeling that you communicate when you ask for referrals are more important than the exact words you use. Oh sure, *what* you say is important. You need to make sense, communicate clearly and make sure you are understood. But what you are communicating on a feeling level is much more significant in terms of how other people will respond to you.

If you talk to someone and you get the sense they are sincere and they treat you with honor and respect, are you more likely to continue to listen to what they have to say? Probably.

If you believe in a salesperson and feel she has her heart in the right place, yet she stumbles through asking you to introduce her to people you know, would you want to help her out? Probably.

If you talk to someone and you get the sense that they are reading a script, or they start telling you what you need, or you start to feel like your thoughts and feelings are not important, are you going to want to continue the conversation? Probably not. Does it matter how good the offer is or how articulate the salesperson is if you are turned off by the values and attitude of the salesperson? Probably not.

Saying the words exactly right is *not* the most important part of asking for referrals. It is *who you are being* when you ask. It is *what you feel* when you ask. It is what your clients feel as a result of what *you* are feeling when you ask for their help. Get clear about what it feels like to be who you want to be, and most any language will work.

PART THREE
Building a Referral Track

THE BUILDING BLOCKS

We have defined the main obstacles in the way of asking for referrals and presented some proven solutions. It's time to develop some referral language, or a *referral language track*. Like the track that keeps a train rolling along to its destination, the referral language track has a similar function. It is a guideline for what to say. There are different options that you can use or not use depending on the situation and what your intuitive instincts tell you to do. You can learn your referral language track word for word or you can ad-lib. But you need to know the basic message you are trying to get across.

Even though your overall attitude is more important than the exact words you use, it is still important to communicate clearly. There are a lot of ways to say things, but no matter how you say it, the communication needs to be clear. What I have found is that you will be more effective if you *get a feel* for what you want to say and then let the words flow from your mind. Some people like specific language and always say about the same thing. Some people like specific language to start out with and then once they have used the language a few times, they tend to wing it. And finally, there is a group of people who get a sense or feel for what they want to say and let the words come out however they do, and rarely say the same thing twice. All of these approaches work equally well as long as you put them into practice.

What follows is an overview of several steps that can be included in a referral language track. The key is to find the sequence of steps and the specific language that feel right to you and then give it a try. I have marked a number of steps as optional. In a way, every step is optional except for actually asking for referrals. Some people make it that simple. Some salespeople like to explain the process in more detail. Again, it doesn't matter how you do it, only that it feels right to you. Because if it feels right, you will be more comfortable asking people to introduce you to people they know, and they will be more willing to help you. Remember, there is no such thing as referral language that works every time.

When Is the Best Time to Ask?

When is the best time to ask for referrals? The conventional wisdom says: whenever the prospect or client is feeling good about you, the work you are doing, or the work you have done. This is often at the time of delivery of the product or service if the sales process requires several calls. If you are in a one-call close situation, the time to ask is when people have made a positive decision or have demonstrated in some way that they like you, your product, or your service.

I have heard people say, "Ask for referrals every chance you get!" This can certainly work if you are comfortable with this approach. However, I think you will agree after reading this material that you are going to get higher-quality referrals if you have established some kind of relationship with your prospect before you ask.

It also depends on what you are asking for. Most people are going to want to get to know you before they will risk referring you to their friends. However, they might be more willing to introduce you to a business associate if what you're offering has a strong enough appeal. If you are asking people to simply identify who they know who may have a need for a product or service you are offering, and it is understood that you are not going to use their name, you may get some cooperation. But this kind of an introduction is more a qualified lead than a referral, since you are not using a nominator's name.

Get a Positive Affirmation

If you miss the magic moment to ask for referrals, which can happen for any number of reasons, all is not lost. You can create a positive atmosphere in which to ask for referrals by asking your client what he has liked about you and the work you have done. This is called getting a *positive affirmation* from your client.

For example, you are talking to your client, Jim, who has purchased your product or service after several meetings.

You: "Jim, let me ask you a question. What have you liked about the work we have done together?"

Jim: "I thought you did a nice job. You helped us clarify our thinking and get a plan in place that makes sense to us."

Give Them a Way Out

Assuming that Jim's feedback was positive, you could continue by asking Jim for a favor and most important, *give him a way out*. The most powerful way to demonstrate to your clients that you are not of the dominance and control school of thought is to always give them options and then let them choose for themselves. This means that regardless of what *you* think they should do, you always give them a clear opportunity to make their own decision. In this way, you honor them as people. You honor *their* wants, needs and desires by allowing *them* to choose what feels right to them.

When you are asking for referrals, you give people a way out by using language like this:

You: "Jim, I would like to ask you for your help ... but with one condition."

Jim: "Yes, what's that?"

You: "The condition is that I only want your help if you are comfortable helping me. Does that sound fair?"

Jim: "Sure, how can I help you?"

You have given Jim a way out by not demanding that he help you or inferring that he should. He doesn't have to help you unless he is comfortable doing so. Jim appreciates your consideration and is now listening for how he can help you. At this point, you can go into an explanation of why referrals are important to your business, followed by how the process typically works.

Explain How the Process Works

Now your objective is to explain to the client what you are asking for, why it is important to you, and how the process works. This is a minisale in the sense that you want to make the process as easy as possible for your clients and assure them that this is a safe process for all involved. You will not embarrass your nominator in any way and will honor the people he introduces you to by treating them with respect. The following is some language that has worked for me personally and that I know hundreds of my coaching clients have used with great success.

You: "What I have found is that my best source of business usually comes from being introduced to people like yourself; the same way I was introduced to you by your friend Larry [delete this sentence if not true]. I am not looking for people who are in the market to buy anything. I simply want to meet people. People like yourself who are doing well and appreciate knowing about constructive ways to get the most out of the money they earn."

"I like to make the introduction process as easy as possible for everyone involved. What I do is send out this letter with your name at the bottom in bold [show client]. Frankly, what the letter says isn't as important as having your name at the bottom. With your name on this letter, I will get in to see most people for a few minutes out of courtesy to you. And that is all I want, just a few minutes to introduce myself and say hello. The rest of the conversation is up to them."

Would You Be Comfortable?

At this point, it's time to ask your client if she is comfortable with your approach. You ask the question and then be quiet.

Don't give in to the temptation to answer the question for your client, or try to make the situation more comfortable for her. Be quiet and wait for a response and pay attention. You need to determine what your client is actually saying. If she says "Sure, I would be happy to help you," you are off and rolling. However, what often happens is that people will give you less than a clear response. You have to determine if their response is one that just needs some minor encouragement, or if they really mean no.

If someone says to you, "Let me talk to a few people first," sometimes this can work. Ask when you can get back to her and follow up. Most often, this isn't a very promising response since it is usually a "disguised no" because the client is hoping that you will forget to follow up. Or the client can indefinitely say that she has not had a chance to bring up the matter with her friends. Often with this response, your client is hoping you will either lose interest in asking her for referrals or get busy with other things and forget about her altogether. Some people have a difficult time saying no, and will never say it.

Some people will say, "Let me think about that a little bit." This is often a tough one to read. You can come back with something like: "I would be happy to give you some time. I guess the main thing I want to know is if you would be comfortable introducing me to people. Because if that is something you typically don't do, I will understand. Would you be open to the idea of introducing me to people you know?"

You have asked the same question again to see if you can flush out more information. If your client's response is still "Let me give it some thought," that is most likely a "disguised no." At this point, I would ask her how she would like to proceed. You could say, "When should I get back to you on this?" Again listen for her response. If she seems hesitant again, you may have someone who could be a good client and is uncomfortable telling you she doesn't want to introduce you to anyone.

You have to be able to read between the lines of the responses you get. You know that "no" doesn't necessarily mean "no." That is often people's first response, no matter what you are proposing. So you may want to give them another chance. The most important thing is that you don't want to present yourself as pushing for referrals or demanding anything. However, you do want to know if this is something they would be comfortable doing because it would mean a lot to you. At the same time, you honor their feelings on the subject and if they are not comfortable introducing you for any reason, no more needs to be said. This is a legitimate conversation to have. You need to know where they stand because you don't want to be a pest. However, a reality of business is that being introduced is the most effective way to do business in most cases, so this is a conversation you need to have with your clients.

Some sample language could sound like this:

You: "Would you be comfortable having me send this letter
to some of the people you know?"

Or, if you are not using a letter:

You: "Would you be willing to introduce me to people on
this basis?"

Focus with Categories

Now you have another choice to make. If your client says he
would be willing to help you and gives you a few names, you
can leave it at that. However, you may find it useful to help
your client focus in on the type of person you are interested in
meeting.

One approach is to determine what qualities the kind of people you want to meet would have, and then add those qualities
to the question "Who do you know who ..." Let's say you
want to meet people who are earning above-average incomes:

- Who do you know who is doing well?
- Who do you know who owns their own business?
- Who do you know who just got a promotion?
- Who do you expect to do really well in the next
  couple of years?

Qualify

Qualifying the referred leads you get can save you a lot of
time, especially if you are getting more referred leads than
you have time to call on. This may sound somewhat optimistic
if you have not been asking for referrals and would be happy

to be able to limit your prospecting calls to "referrals only." The reality is, many salespeople don't have time to get to all the people they have been introduced to. Whatever your situation, you will have to decide what kind of information you want to get about the names your client gives you. One of the most effective approaches is to ask your client what he likes about the people he is introducing you to.

You: "Jim, what do you like about Fred?"

Jim: "Fred is a sharp guy. He has a lot of good business sense and he has been a good friend."

You: "Would you mind if I told him what you just said?"

Jim: "Sure, you can tell him that."

Two wonderful things happen with this approach. First, Jim is now more excited about you calling his friend Fred because Jim is going to look good when you tell Fred the good things Jim has said. Second, when you call Fred on the telephone, you can open with something like:

You: "Fred, I was talking to Jim Moore the other day and he had some very complimentary things to say about you ..."

Fred: "Oh, he did, did he?"

You: "Yes, Jim said you were a very sharp businessman and a good friend, and he felt you and I would enjoy meeting and that's why I'm calling ..."

All Together Now

The following is the referral language just presented, put together so you can see it all at once.

(GET A POSITIVE AFFIRMATION.)

You: "Jim, let me ask you a question. What have you liked about the work we have done together?"

Jim: "I thought you did a nice job. You helped us clarify our thinking and get a plan in place that makes sense to us."

(GIVE THEM A WAY OUT.)

You: "Well, Jim, I would like to ask you for your help ... but with one condition."

Jim: "Yes, what's that?"

You: "The condition is that I only want your help if you are comfortable helping me. Does that sound fair?"

Jim: "Sure, how can I help you?"

(EXPLAIN HOW THE PROCESS WORKS.)

You: "What I have found is that my best source of business usually comes from being introduced to people like yourself; the same way I was introduced to you by your friend Larry [delete this sentence if not true].

I am not looking for people who are in the market to

buy anything. I simply want to meet people; people like yourself who are doing well and appreciate knowing about constructive ways to get the most out of the money they earn.

I like to make the introduction process as easy as possible for everyone involved. What I do is send out this letter with your name at the bottom in bold [show client]. Frankly, what the letter says isn't as important as having your name at the bottom. With your name on this letter, I will get in to see most people for a few minutes out of courtesy to you. And that is all I want, just a few minutes to introduce myself and say hello. The rest of the conversation is up to them."

(*WOULD YOU BE COMFORTABLE?*)

You: "Would you be comfortable having me send this letter to some of the people you know?"

Or, if you are not using a letter:

You: "Would you be willing to introduce me to people on this basis?"

(*FOCUS WITH CATEGORIES.*)

You: "Who do you know who is doing well? Who do you know who owns their own business? Who do you know who just got a promotion?"

(*QUALIFY.*)

You: "Jim, what do you like about Fred?"

Jim: "Fred is a sharp guy. He has a lot of good business sense and he has been a good friend."

You: "Would you mind if I told him what you just said?"

Jim: "Sure, you can tell him that."

BUSINESS & PROFESSIONAL SAMPLE LANGUAGE

This language has a different beginning. Instead of getting a positive affirmation and asking for a favor up front, we change the order and add a new perspective. This approach is designed to get a business owner to agree that his best source of new business is some form of referral and then tell him that the same is true in your business.

You: "Tim, let me ask you a question. What would you say is your best source of new business?"

Tim: "Referrals, satisfied customers, being introduced by clients [any of these will work]."

You: "The same is true in my business, and I would like to ask for your help but with one condition ..."

Tim: "What's that?"

You: "I would like to ask for your help, but only if you are comfortable introducing me to people. If you're not comfortable, I will understand and no more needs to be said. But before you make a decision, let me show you how I like to be introduced.

I like to make it as easy as possible for everyone involved. What I do is send out this letter with your name at the bottom [show client] and frankly, what the letter says isn't as important as having your name at the bottom. With your name on this letter, I will get in to see most people for a few minutes. And that is all I want, just to introduce myself and say hello. The rest of the conversation is up to them.

Does that sound like a fair approach?

Would you be comfortable having me send this letter to people you know?"

Tim: "I can probably think of a few names for you."

You: "Thanks Tim. Let me give you an idea of the kind of person I am looking for. Who do you know who …?"

KEEPER PHRASES

Everyone is going to ask for referrals a little differently. As you get more comfortable with the process of asking for referrals, you will find yourself saying things that you really like and that really seem to work for you. Don't be concerned if you have never heard anyone use a certain phrase. All that matters is that the phrase works for you. I like to call these expressions "keeper phrases." The following is a list of a few phrases that some of my clients have blended into the referral talks.

"Without your influence, I am nothing but a stranger."

"I will get in to see people because your name is on the bottom of this page."

"I promise you I won't embarrass you in any way. I will spend 10 minutes, introduce myself, tell them a little about what I do, and be gone."

"Most people are not in the market right now. Often there is a year or two lead time before someone becomes a client. I just want the opportunity to put my 'hat in the ring' for their future business."

"I am looking for people I can meet and get to know so when they *are* in the market, I will have a good chance at getting their business."

"I would like to have met them and know them so they will think of me when they are ready to do something."

"I simply want to introduce myself and get their thinking on a couple of ideas. I haven't found a person yet who wasn't comfortable with that approach."

"With your permission only, I would like to show them a couple of ways they can save money on their _____."

"I will take no more than 10 minutes to introduce myself and share a couple of ideas on _____. If they want to continue the conversation or get back together, that will be totally up to them."

"What I have found is that when I meet people, either the chemistry is there or it isn't. If the chemistry is there, we will probably do business at some point. If the chemistry is not there, we will at least have met and we could be a potential resource to one another at a later time."

Collect the phrases you like and insert them into your language at the appropriate spot. Even more important, listen for the things you say that you really like when you ask for referrals. You may surprise yourself. I have actually coached people to develop highly effective sales language in this way. I have them get a general idea of what they want to say but nothing very specific. Then I have them make 10 to 20 telephone calls and record the calls. The goal is to identify and repeat the things they said that they liked and seemed to work. Then you collect these phrases until you have your telephone language. This approach may sound a bit unorthodox, but it is extremely effective for developing language that really fits you. The challenge, of course, is to make calls while not knowing exactly what you are going to say and being willing to not care what happens on a few calls while you are creating your language.

QUANTITY VS. QUALITY

Once you have identified the people who are willing to help you, there is another decision to make. Some salespeople prefer to get only the names of the referror's closest friends and associates. What works for other salespeople is to get as many names as they can get. Whatever your expectation is, that's probably what you will get. I have seen salespeople send out a sheet of paper with spaces for the names, addresses, and telephone numbers of 30 people and get them back completely filled in.

If you are looking for a lot of names, you can get your clients thinking bigger and hint about how many names you are looking for by saying something like:

You: "You know, Jim, they say that most people know from 500 to 1,000 people. Obviously I don't expect to be introduced to 500 people, but at the same time, I don't want you to feel limited in any way. I am interested in sending out letters to as many people as you feel comfortable giving me. Let me tell you a little bit more about the kind of person I am looking for ..."

GO BACK TO THE WELL

Again, once you have identified people who are willing to help you, this doesn't mean you are limited to asking for referrals just one time. There are people who are constantly meeting new people. Ask your referrors if you can check back with them periodically to find out if they have met anyone interesting.

Take care of the people who are willing to help you. Send thank-you cards. Let them know about the successes you have with the people they know (don't bring up the others, if possible). In some cases, you may want to do more than send a thank-you card. This is a judgment call on your part. Some people are uncomfortable receiving any kind of gift for the help they have given you. Most often people are pleasantly surprised and appreciative of gifts. You have to decide what's appropriate for your business and the level of the relationship. A gift that is too extravagant can easily make people uncomfortable. Keep it simple and of meaning to them, if possible. Find out what their favorite restaurant is and buy them a gift certificate. Any kind of consumable item works well as a gift. Do some investigating to find out what they like and give them a modest amount. Remember, it's the thought and effort on your part that count more than how much you spend. The next time you see your referring clients, listen carefully to determine how the gift was received. If you get a clearly positive response, you can do something for them again if the situation presents itself. Otherwise, stick to a thank-you note. I have never heard of anyone feeling uncomfortable about getting a thank-you note.

ASK YOUR PEERS WHAT'S WORKING FOR THEM

How someone asks for referrals is not a competitive threat to most salespeople. Therefore, if you ask your peers or even leaders in your company how they ask for referrals, they will most often be very cooperative. Remember that what works for someone else may not work for you, and that whatever you use should feel right to you. Do some research, collect some ideas, and give them a try. Keep the ones that you like the most and that seem to work.

I worked with a life insurance agent who got over 1,000 referrals in one year and wrote business on over 400 of those people in the same year. I asked him where he got his language. He said he got every word from articles written by his peers in trade magazines. Find out what your peers are doing and then customize whatever you use to fit your values, personality, and style.

A LETTER REQUESTING REFERRALS

Sometimes it's appropriate to request referrals with a letter. The following letter includes many of the ideas presented thus far:

Date

Will U. Referme
Network, Inc.
40 Prospect Court
Point, ME 22000

Dear Will:

I'm writing this letter to ask for your help ... but with one condition. The condition is that I only want your help if you are comfortable doing so. I have found that my best source of new business comes from being introduced to people by my friends and clients. I am not looking for people who are in the market to buy anything at this time. I am simply looking for people who appreciate hearing about constructive ways to get the most out of the money they earn.

I like to make the introduction process as easy as possible for everyone involved. What I do is send out the enclosed letter with your name in bold at the bottom. Frankly, what the letter says isn't as important as having your name on it. With your name at the bottom, I will get to meet over 95% of the people I call. Without a name, the percentage goes down considerably. So you can see that being introduced in this way makes a huge difference in my effectiveness and time management.

When I meet people for the first time, I like to keep the meeting short. I mainly want to have a chance to introduce myself and get to know each other for a few minutes. If they find something interesting in what I have to say and want to meet with me again, that's up to them. Either way, I like to be a resource to the people I meet, knowing that some of them will become clients in the future.

Would you be willing to have me send my letter to some of the people you know? In most cases, people won't bother to call you to ask about me. They will simply give me a few minutes out of courtesy to you and leave it at that. If someone does call you to ask about me, I am mainly asking for a character reference. Just tell them I am a good person worth talking to for a few minutes.

I will give you a call in a few days to find out if you would be comfortable introducing me on this basis.

Sincerely,

Your Name Here

PART FOUR
Contacting the Referral

CONTACTING THE REFERRAL

There are a number of ways to contact your referrals once you have successfully acquired their names. Any of the following have worked well for many salespeople:

- Send them a letter on your letterhead.
- Send them a note.
- Send a letter on "monarch" stationery or something more personal-looking.
- Have the referror write the note or letter.
- Send the referral a letter or note from you with a note from your referror on it.
- Send the referral a letter with the referror's name at the bottom in bold in the P.S.
- Send the referral a letter with your hand-written P.S. at the bottom with the referror's name in it.
- Send a letter mentioning the referror in the body of the letter, in bold.
- Call your referral on the telephone.
- Have your referror call the referrals while you are in his office.

There are numerous options. You have to decide what works best for you.

I have alluded to my preference for making the process as simple as possible for everyone involved. I like letters with people's names at the bottom in the P.S. Hundreds of my clients say that this approach works extremely well and agree that it's one of the easiest approaches for all concerned.

WHAT DO YOU SAY IN A LETTER

Whether you are writing a note or a letter to a referral, there are several things you should consider including:

Talk benefits. Make a list of all the benefits of your product or service. Then pick the top one or two benefits and make sure you get these benefits clearly stated in the letter. Too often salespeople talk in terms of features without enough benefits. A good test to determine whether you have a strong enough benefit is to ask, "What's the benefit in the long run?" after each statement describing what you do for people. For example, "I help people organize their finances." So what's the long range benefit of having your finances organized? You will be more likely to reach your financial goals. You will have greater peace of mind knowing an organized plan is in place.

"We help people make educated decisions that feel right to them." What is the long-range benefit? It may be implied but not clearly enough stated. Instead you could say, "We help people make educated decisions that feel right to them so they end up with a program that will accomplish their long-range objectives." You don't have to have a long-range benefit in every sentence of your letter. Make sure you state your biggest long-range benefits clearly and ideally in the first sentence of your letter.

Give them a way out. Letters that give your referrals a way out are much more powerful than demanding that they meet with you. If I say to you, "You need to hear what I have to say," what image or feeling comes to mind? Probably something like, "Who does this guy think he is?" It is much more powerful and inviting to say something like, "I have no reason to believe you are currently in the market for _____." Or, "I have no way of knowing if you are currently a candidate for _____."

Give them a reputation to live up to. Giving your referrals a reputation to live up to means saying something nice about them. For example, "You have been described to me as someone who is interested in constructive ideas." Or, "Joe said you have a keen business sense and I would like to get your opinion on a new service we are offering our preferred clients."

Promise to be brief. Your referrals will be much more receptive to meeting you if you have promised not to take up too much of their time. This gives them a chance to check you out to see if there is enough interest or chemistry to continue pursuing a relationship. You could say something like, "I promise to be brief and that any subsequent meetings will be at your request." Or, "I would like to meet with you for no more than 15 minutes and promise to be brief and to the point."

Mention your referror's name. Psychological research has shown that people's attention will quickly go to a postscript or "P.S." at the end of a letter. Typically, a letter with a P.S. will be quickly scanned and then the P.S. will get the first serious attention. Therefore, the P.S. is a smart place to put your referror's name, and in bold. Other studies have shown that what people see first and last has the greatest impact. Two sample letters follow using both approaches.

SAMPLE LETTERS

Sample Letter 1 is a modified version of an idea I got from Hugh Thompson in 1975. Hugh Thompson is one of the all-time greats in the life insurance business. When I met him, he was traveling the country sharing some of his most successful approaches for selling life insurance. I have found this letter to be extremely effective both for me and for hundreds of my financial services clients.

Sample Letter 2 has a little different format. The referral's name is mentioned twice in the body of the letter instead of the P.S.: once in bold in the first sentence and again in the last sentence. Both letters have some version of the five parts described in the previous section.

Sample Letter 1
(Your Letterhead)

Date

Person U. Wannameet
241 Prospect Court
Anytown, US 54321

Dear Person:

Within the next few days, I will be contacting you to ask your permission to meet with you at your convenience. I have no reason to believe you are presently interested in equity investments or insurance planning, but you have been described to me as a person who is interested in constructive ideas.

My ideas involve ways to maximize your "before-tax" income. I assure you that I will be brief and that subsequent meetings will be arranged at your request. I will not attempt to sell you any products during this interview. I simply want to meet you and share some information that has been very valuable to many people like yourself. I hope that we can get together on this basis.

Sincerely,

Will U. Follow-up
WUF/bhs

P.S. Prior to my calling, you may want to refer to **Tom Cruise** regarding me and the type of service I offer.

Sample Letter 2
(Your Letterhead)

Date

Person U. Wannameet
241 Prospect Court
Anytown, US 54321

Dear Person:

I recently had the pleasure of meeting and doing some work for **Paul and Jamie Buchmann**. In the process of our conversation, your name was mentioned as a leader in your field who is open to new and constructive ideas.

My service is designed to _____. [Lots of benefits here.] I promise to be brief and that subsequent meetings will be at your request.

I will give you a call within a week or so to arrange a convenient time to meet you and introduce myself. In the interim, if you have any questions about me or my service, please don't hesitate to give Paul and Jamie a call.

Kind regards,

Will U. Follow-up

WUF/bhs

WHAT DO YOU SAY ON THE TELEPHONE?

Some people don't want to take the time or trouble to send a letter. They like to get on the telephone and call. Sending a letter first doesn't necessarily work better than simply calling people with no introduction. You have to discover what approach works best for you.

Calling a referral on the telephone is like any other kind of telephone sales call. You want to be upbeat and sound like someone who is enjoying life, someone who would be interesting to meet. What you say is secondary to how you feel when you say it. If you are feeling relaxed and confident with a genuine desire to meet new people, this will come through in your voice. If you can, give people a reputation to live up to by telling them the good things their referror said about them. If you don't want to quote the referror, make a general complimentary statement about them.

Keep it simple. Talk in terms of the general benefits of your product or service. Don't get into too much detail over the telephone. Your main objective is to get an appointment with people who are open to having one. The most significant difference when calling a referral is that you have a name you can use and you want to mention the referror's name right away. Your language could be something like this:

Sample Language 1

You: "Jim, this is _____. We have not met, but I was talking with John Garrison recently and he had some very complimentary things to say about you. [Pause]

Jim: "Oh, is that right?"

You: "Yes, as a matter of fact, he said you were a very sharp businessman and that you and I should have a chance to meet. And that's why I'm calling. I wanted to see if we could get together for a few minutes next week so I can introduce myself in person and tell you a little bit about the kind of work I do [or tell you a little bit about my _____ service or tell you a little bit about my new line of _____.]"

Sample Language 2

You: "Jim, this is Sid Walker. Do you have a minute to talk?"

Tim: "I've just got a couple of minutes before I have to go out."

You: "That's fine. I will keep it short. I was talking to our mutual friend, Larry Johnson, the other day and he had some very good things to say about you."

Tim: [Pauses, doesn't say anything.]

You: [With a smile.] "You know Larry, don't you?"

Tim: "Oh, sure, I know him. Larry is a good friend."

You: "Well, Larry thought that you and I would enjoy meeting and that's why I'm calling ..."

Sample Language 3

You: "I was talking to a friend of yours recently, Cathy Hubbard."

Kay: "Oh, sure. I know Cathy."

You: "Cathy had some very complimentary things to say about you and one of those things was that you are open to new ideas on how to save money on your _____, and that's also the reason for my call. I was wondering if we might be able to get together for a few minutes next week so I can formally introduce myself.

Kay: "What do you do?"

You: "I am in the _____ business. A lot of the work I do is focused on helping people _____. I am not calling with the idea that you are in the market for _____. Cathy felt you and I would enjoy meeting each other and I was hoping you might have a few minutes next week. Can you squeeze me in?"

Remember, your objective is to attempt to get an appointment, not to get into the sales process over the telephone. At the same time, if your referred prospect is clearly not interested and you sense a meeting would be a waste of time after a couple of attempts to connect with him or her, move on to the next prospect. Most people are naturally a little cautious talking to someone they don't know. However, you can sense if you are getting a weak excuse that just needs some additional encouragement on your part or if your referred prospect is truly not interested.

WHAT TO DO WHEN YOU GET THERE

I have written a book on what to do in a sales interview. The book is entitled *How to Double Your Sales by Asking a Few More Questions*. Also, in the appendix of my first book, *Trusting Yourself*, I have written out a comprehensive first-interview track that has been highly successful for many hundreds of my clients and for my own sales efforts as well. The following are overviews of what to do in the first interview from both books.

An Overview of the Sales Process

- Start with "small talk."

- Give a general statement of benefit describing what you do.

- Give a purpose for the meeting, what to expect.

- Get permission to ask questions: "Jim, so I can make sure I am talking about things that are of interest to you, could I ask you a few questions?"

- Move to easy questions that are directly or indirectly related to your product or service — questions relating to what their experience has been with your product or service. What have they done? How much do they know? What do they like? What do they dislike?

- Tell them the three things people like most about your product or service and then ask them which one would be most important to them and why that would be important.

- Or, show them a "menu" of benefits related to the problems your product or service addresses.

- Find out which item(s) is most important and *why* it's important.

- Show how your product or service gives them what they want.

An Overview of Who to Be

- Be "in partnership" with your clients. Get on their side of the table and help them make the decision that feels right to them.

- Create rapport by finding things in common with your prospects.

- Don't hesitate to share your own experience to get people to open up.

- Take a sincere interest in your prospect. Ask lots of questions and listen carefully to what they have to say.

- Summarize and clarify what they want by repeating things back in their own words.

- Be safe to talk to by being nonjudgmental of their answers.

- Imagine the ideal qualities of the kind of person you would want to work with and demonstrate those qualities.

CHEMISTRY AND TIMING

In my 16 years as a peak performance coach, two concepts clearly stand out as the most effective ways to substantially increase sales production. One concept is getting the prospect or client to the feeling level in the interview. This is a process of getting your prospects to verbalize on a feeling level, why something is important to them. I have detailed this process in my book *How to Double Your Sales by Asking a Few More Questions*. The second concept is what I call the *Chemistry and Timing Formula*.

Chemistry describes a good feeling that you have for another person. You like each other. You respect each other. You seem to get along. You have things in common. Some combination of these qualities is what is often referred to as *chemistry* between two people. *Timing* means that your prospect has a current need for the product or service you are offering.

Then, the question you have to ask yourself is: Would you be willing to consider that chemistry and timing are actually required to make a sale today? When was the last time you made a sale where the chemistry and timing were not there? Most salespeople today will agree that the most empowering approach for all involved is when the chemistry and timing are right.

What the Chemistry and Timing Formula states is that if the chemistry is there in the first meeting, you continue to work with this prospect. If you determine that the chemistry is not there, you don't pursue the relationship. If the chemistry is there and the timing isn't (no current need for your product or service), you put the prospect back in your tickler file for a later call.

You are not going to be 100% accurate in your judgment of people. You will walk away from some sales you could have made with the Chemistry and Timing Formula. However, my research and the hindsight of many of my clients make a very strong case for the Chemistry and Timing approach. What salespeople typically discover is that substantial increases in income, and the sense of well-being that comes from working with people you enjoy having a relationship with, far outweigh a few missed sales with more difficult people.

What if you can't determine if the chemistry is there or not in the first meeting? This is a judgment call on your part. Sometimes it is difficult to read people in just one meeting. If it feels right, go back for another meeting. If at any point you your intuitive instincts are telling you that something isn't right or the relationship just seems to be too much effort, let it go and get on to someone new.

I coach a lot of very successful experienced salespeople who are unfortunately also very burned out. One of my first questions to these people is, "Do you like your clients?" Guess what their answer often is? "A few of them!" They didn't think they had a choice about who they worked with. Many have spent 20 years or more working with people they would love not to have to deal with. But they thought that was just part of the job. Experienced salespeople who switch to the Chemistry and Timing Formula regularly tell me they wish they would have had this information 20 years ago. Their careers would have been very different.

PART FIVE
Alternate Approaches

DEVELOPING CENTERS OF INFLUENCE

Centers of Influence are people who will refer business to you. They can be clients, but they don't have to be. They might refer one prospect to you or they might refer prospects to you on a regular, ongoing basis. They simply need to believe in what you do enough to want to refer people to you.

Often a Center of Influence is a third party that comes into contact with the type of people you want to meet. In the financial services industry, these include accountants, attorneys, and bank or trust officers who are in a position to refer their wealthy clients. Many of the biggest producers in the life insurance and investment business get their leads from third-party Centers of Influence. A great deal of time and money are spent courting these Centers of Influence with the hope of establishing enough of a relationship and enough credibility that you get a call when they need the type of services you offer.

Many salespeople attempt to develop relationships with Centers of Influence by inviting them to breakfast or lunch and showing them the kind of work they do. This works to some degree. You may have to talk to a lot of people to find the few people you really have chemistry with and who believe in your ability. Centers of Influence can be a very conservative group since they usually have a strong relationship with their client and they don't want to refer their client to anyone they are not very sure about. So you have to establish your credibility and professionalism.

Sample Interview Language

In addition to establishing credibility by showing potential Centers of Influence what you do, you can speed up the relationship-building process by asking a few questions. The following is a sample of some of the questions you could ask:

You: "Will, I appreciate the opportunity to meet with you today and show you some of the things that I have been able to do for my clients. Would it be okay if I asked you a couple of additional questions?"

Will: "Sure."

You: "Do you ever refer business out to _____ (your profession)?"

Will: "Occasionally. A lot depends on the situation."

You: "Of course. What do you like to see in order to be comfortable referring business to people in my profession?"

Will: "Oh, we like to see a successful track record of experience in the specific area where we need help. We also like to see some _____."

You: "If a person had these qualifications ... [summarize and repeat qualifications using their words], how would that help you and your client in the long run?

(If you are uncomfortable asking the last question, get a copy of my book *How to Double Your Sales by Asking a Few More Questions*. Sure, it's a question with an obvious answer and there are two things to remember. The first is that if you are in rapport with your Centers of Influence, they will be happy to answer the question. People love to be interviewed. The second is, when the Center of Influence verbalizes why the qualifications are important, the relationship will go to a much deeper level, which is what you need with a Center of Influence to get referrals. There is no guarantee that you will get referrals from Centers of Influence if you ask these questions.

But it is very likely that you won't get any referrals if you don't ask them.)

Will: "I think that the most important thing we are looking for is people we can trust to get the job done right and make us look good in the process."

You: "I understand. [Pause to collect your thoughts.] Will, if I could meet the qualifications you have listed here and, most important, be the kind of person your company could trust to get the job done right, and, as you say, make you look good, would you be willing to consider me as a resource for your clients?"

Will: "Sure, we would certainly keep you in mind if something came up that was a match."

You: "Will, over the past twelve months or so, how many opportunities would you say you have had to refer business to someone like myself?"

Will: "Probably several times a year." [Will's answer will tell you what kind of potential there is for referrals. If he says once every five years, you had better keep looking for more Centers of Influence.]

You: "Will, one other important question. I am sure you have relationships with other people like myself. What would it take for me to get on the short list of people you refer business too?" [Don't ask this question if it makes you uncomfortable. However, if you want to find out where you stand, ask this question and then listen carefully.]

You: "Thank you, Will. I appreciate this opportunity to explore the possibility of being a resource to each other. Let's talk for a minute about how I might be able to make your job a little easier ..."

This is probably the most involved you are going to get a Center of Influence in an initial conversation. The power of the questions is that you get to demonstrate your problem-solving ability by asking the questions. Your Center of Influence gets to verbalize what's important to him and why. Your Center also knows you know what's important to him because you asked the questions and listened to his answers. You then summarized what he said was important, and asked him if you fulfilled all of the qualifications, would he consider you as a resource for the right situation. You have very effectively gotten across to your Center of Influence what you want and you have involved him in a very meaningful way. He will remember you in a positive light.

Be a Resource

Being a resource to your Centers of Influence *before* you get any referrals is important to help build the relationship and establish your credibility. Let your Centers know what types of information or services you can offer them that could help them get their work done more effectively or more easily. Find out what kinds of information or services would be useful to the Center personally. What topics do they like to be kept up-to-date on. Develop the reputation for being current on key issues.

Being Visible to Potential Centers of Influence

There are lots of ways to get your name in front of potential Centers of Influence. You can write articles in their trade publications. Send out newsletters. Send out postcards with announcements of important upcoming events. You could host a golf tournament or sports outing. Host a luncheon and bring in a speaker on a current topic of interest to your potential Centers. Speak to their associations. Write pamphlets, special reports, or books on subjects that will be popular with the people you want to refer you business. With computer technology today, writing and publishing professional-looking material is relatively easy. Besides, you don't have to write a 200-page book and get published by a major publisher to get the attention of your potential Centers of Influence. Most professional people have too much to read already and appreciate publications that are short and to the point on timely subjects.

Basically, any way you can get known as an expert in your field will contribute to the clout you will have in developing Centers of Influence.

Get Referred to Potential Centers of Influence

Your client's advisors can be a bountiful source of potential Centers of Influence. My wife, Linda, who is a money manager, recently reminded me that most of her business in recent years has come from Centers of Influence.

She asks her clients who their accountant and attorney are. Then she asks her clients if she can introduce herself to the accountant and attorney as the client's money manager. If a client says "sure," then Linda calls these Centers of Influence and meets with them to learn more about what they do, and to show them her type of work. This approach has created many Centers of Influence for Linda and a large number of her current clients.

Since you already have a relationship with your clients, it is very natural to ask to meet their other advisors. Furthermore, both you and the advisors you are being introduced to have the same client in common. The initial rapport level of this type of meeting is usually very strong and most often will result in both more contacts and more business.

THE GOLF APPROACH

Golf is such an effective way to network with potential clients that many people have taken up the game just for this purpose. Golf is a very social, slow-moving game. You spend four-five hours with no more than three other people. You are going to get to know a lot about each other.

Many people like to meet potential business contacts on the golf course because it gives them a chance to really get to see how people operate in a nonbusiness setting. You get to watch how a person responds to the challenges of the game. Do they stay cool under pressure or do they lose their temper and swear a lot? Do they seem organized and deliberate in their strategy toward the game, or do they fly by the seat of their pants hoping for the best? How people handle themselves on the golf course is likely how they are going to handle your business.

Of my over 1,500 individual life insurance clients, many are skilled golfers and many use golf as a way to do big business. Following are some guidelines for using golf as a way to get introduced to new people.

• You call a friend, associate, or client and ask him to bring two people that have the potential to be good clients. You want to make sure you tell him what you are looking for. I have a client named George who decided to take this approach and told one of his clients to bring two other people to play. His friend brought his 13-year-old son and one of his son's friends. They had a good round of golf, but not much potential for new business, at least not for 15 to 20 years!

I have another avid golfer client that shared an approach that has been extremely effective for him. You invite a CPA or an attorney to play a round of golf. Then you tell him to bring someone that would be a good potential person for you to meet and you will bring someone that would be good for the CPA or attorney to meet.

- You pick up the expenses for your guests. You have to decide if you want to pick up all expenses or most of them. The expenses can include any combination of the following: greens fees, lunch, cart, caddie, drinks afterward, or dinner depending on the time of day you play.

- You don't discuss business unless your guest brings it up, and then be intriguingly vague. You say things like, "That would depend on a number of circumstances." The main rule is to stay away from an in-depth discussion of any business topic. Keep it social.

- Remember you are on stage. People are watching. People are evaluating you and your approach to the game. You want to demonstrate all the qualities on the golf course that you would want people to associate with an astute businessperson. This is also a great excuse to become highly skilled at the game of golf.

- Wait a couple of weeks and give your guests a call. You already know a lot about each other and have met on a very favorable and enjoyable basis. In most cases, they will make time for you.

This is a potentially expensive approach. You have to weigh what the sales potential is for the amount of money you want to spend. If you have told your client, friend, or associate who you want to meet, you will likely end up with guests that will do business. Typically, if you are asking to meet the right people, the business you will do will pay for your investment many times in return. My clients who use this approach tell me it is the most fun part of their practice and their most profitable way to prospect.

You don't have to limit this approach to meeting new people to the golf course. Tell a friend or client that you like to socialize with who you want to meet and set up some kind of social outing. Go out for dinner. Go to a play or the opera and have dinner afterward. Go to a professional sporting event. Anything that allows some time to interact with your guests and get to know each other a little will work. The same guidelines apply as with golf. Let a few weeks go by and then give your new acquaintance a call.

THE INDIVIDUAL SEMINAR APPROACH

The Individual Seminar is unique in that it is *usually a presentation to one person*. It is a concept I have used successfully with a number of my coaching clients. It has been especially effective with those people who have a wealth of technical knowledge and love to teach. The idea is to give a short presentation on a subject you know is of interest to the type of people you want to call on. These calls are typically cold calls in the beginning and, of course, you can use this type of approach with anyone. You could charge for this information, but that tends to complicate the process more than necessary. Keep your presentation to a half-hour. And here is the key: *ask for referrals at the end of each presentation.* You should get enough referrals from your presentations to keep you busy without having to do a lot of cold calling.

What I have found is that if you give people something up front like information that is useful to them, they are usually open to helping you by introducing you to people they know.

At the end of your presentation you can show them a menu of the services you offer and ask if they would be interested in getting additional information on a particular product or service. If you get a positive response, then you are into your usual sales process of fact-finding and presenting solutions to their problems.

When you telephone people, your goal is to be inviting and intriguing. You want to get your prospects' interest and attention with who you are being and what you have to offer. You are operating from a position of strength. You have information to offer that will be useful to your prospects. If they are not interested, you are not going to beg for an appointment. They have to come partway. They have to show some interest. Most people are naturally hesitant to any offer initially. If you don't get a hard "no," tell them what you are doing one more time (in slightly different words) and ask them again if they would be interested. Give them a clear choice and go with whatever they say at this time.

Remember, you are looking for chemistry and timing. If you and your prospect like each other, and what you talk about is of interest to him, he will likely find some way to do business with you in the near future. Even if he doesn't end up doing business with you, he will most likely give you some names of other people to talk to. You will be able to use his name and you will get in to see new people on a very favorable basis.

Sample Opening Language

You: "I help people save substantial amounts of money on
their _____.

And I do this by giving a 25-minute presentation
in your office designed to make you a smarter consumer so you save money now as well as down

the road. There is nothing to buy and there is no charge for this service. My sole purpose at this point is to educate you on what astute people are doing in the _____ area. All I ask is that if you decide to pursue some of my ideas and you are comfortable with me, you will consider doing the business with me.

Does that sound like a fair approach?"

OR

You: "I do a 25-minute presentation in your office on how to determine how much _____ you really need and want, how to pick a good company, and how to spend as little money as possible and still get quality products. Would you be interested in becoming a smarter consumer in these areas?"

Other Language Ideas

"What I do is teach people how to buy _____ in a way that saves them thousands of dollars per year. And I can show you how to do this in about 25 minutes."

"What I do is help people make more and save more money on their _____. I would like to come by your office and show you how I do that. And there's no charge. All I ask is that if you like something I show you, and you like me, that you give me a shot at your business."

"I teach people how to avoid the most common mistakes in the _____ area. Most of the people I talk to feel their time with me was time well spent. I guess the question is, would you be willing to gamble 25 minutes to find out for yourself?"

"I like this way of doing business, because I find most everyone else does. This gives you and me a chance to meet. You
get to see me in action. I will more than pay for the time you
spend with me by showing you how to buy _____
at the right price."

"I will bet that you haven't had an offer this good yet this
year, have you? I am going to come to your office and give
you information most people have to pay for. All I ask is that
if you like me and my ideas, that you give me a shot at some
of your future business. Now that sounds like a fair approach,
doesn't it?!"

Dealing with Initial Resistance

People are naturally suspicious of a good deal. They want to
know the hidden cost. In this case there is no cost other than a
half hour of their time. But you may need to do some gentle
convincing to let people know you are sincere and get them to
take you up on your generous offer.

- **How do you get paid**? The "All I ask ..." language above tends to handle this question, but
  here is another idea: "At some point you will be
  considering buying additional _____.
  I want you to know me well enough that you will
  think of me when you are in the market for my
  kind of service."

- **What are you selling**? "I am not selling anything at this time. If you want to do more with
  me in the future, it will be by mutual consent. At
  this point, I just want to get to know you a little,
  and show you how to put some extra money in
  your pocket, and show you that I know what I'm
  talking about."

- **Can you send me something in the mail**? "I would if I could. Actually, it's going to take me a few minutes to get to know enough about your situation for me to be able to give you some ideas that will be of interest to you. I've found that I can help people a lot more if we meet in person. Can you squeeze me in for 25 minutes next week?"

Lights, Camera, Action

You are at your prospect's office and ready for your presentation. It is usually good to give an overview of what the agenda is going to be. It is also good to get permission to ask a few questions to make sure that the information you are giving them is going to be of interest.

You: "Fred, in order to make sure I'm talking about things that are going to be of interest to you today, would it be okay if I asked you a couple of questions?"

Fred: "Fire away. I'm all yours for the next half hour."

The Menu

A menu is typically a list of the problems that you solve for people with your products or service written in language that presents the strongest benefits. It should be professional-looking. A bulleted list on your letterhead works well. Keep each item to a sentence or two. Then simply place the menu in front of your prospect and ask him to take a minute and read through the list to see if there is anything that is of particular interest or anything he would like to learn more about.

You can use the menu in two ways with the Individual Seminar approach. You can use it in the beginning to focus your discussion. Let your prospect pick the items that are of the most interest. You get permission to ask questions and get some preliminary information. Then you are off and running with your presentation.

The other way to use the menu is at the end of your presentation. Just prior to asking for referrals, show your prospect your menu and ask to take a minute and read through it to see if there is anything he would like to learn more about.

Sample Language Requesting Referrals

You: "Was this information useful to you?"

Joe: "Yes, this has been very informative."

You: "Joe, I wanted to help you a little today, and I also wanted to ask *you* for a favor. Would you be willing to introduce me to three or four people you know that you think would appreciate my approach?"

OR

You: "I wanted to help you out today with some useful information, and I wanted to ask *you* for a favor, but only if you are comfortable helping me. Does that sound fair enough?"

Fred: "Sure. What do you need?"

You: "Would you be comfortable introducing me to three or four people that you know so I could give them a similar presentation?"

Fred: "I think we could manage that for you."

Go out and teach people what they need to know to make more informed decisions related to your product or service. Go demonstrate what it's like to interact with you. Show them your stuff! If the chemistry is there, you will likely do business at some point. You will at least get some referrals. And you will likely do some business with some of the referrals because you will get in on a favorable basis. If the chemistry *and* the timing are there when you meet people, and they often are, you will do some business in the near future with some of these people.

THE NETWORKING APPROACH

People more than ever want to work with people they know, or have at least met, or have some connection with through other people they like. This psychological need to do as much business as we can with people we know has made *networking* an accepted way to approach people you have never met before. Most everyone today realizes the power of a network. The more people you know, the bigger your network. The bigger the network, the greater the resources available to you.

Networking is very social. It is not a sales interview. When you meet with someone with the purpose of networking, you start out with small talk, as you would in any type of interview. Then you usually move to "Tell me about what you do." You both get a chance to talk about your work in a general way. You want to talk in terms of the benefits of your product or service and be as inviting and intriguing as possible.

What you are hoping for is that the person you are talking to will ask you to get her more information on a particular product you have, or ask you how to proceed if she wants to do some work with you. The main difference with a networking interview is that going to the next step of the sales process is not attempted if there is not a clear interest on your prospect's part. There should be no pressure for the other person to get involved in your sales process. She needs to demonstrate to you in some way that she is interested in getting more information. If she doesn't seem to move in your direction, you leave it at that. You can give her one last chance at showing some interest at the end of the interview by asking something like, "I would like you to consider me a resource in the area of _____. Is there any information on a particular product or service that you might have a potential interest in?"

Like the Individual Seminar, a *menu* of the benefits of your services can work well here. You can say: "Here is a list of the type of work I typically do for people. Take a quick look through this list and see if there is anything that looks like it might be of potential interest."

When you network, you're looking for chemistry and any indications of mild interest in your product or service. Some salespeople say they want to take a more direct approach. If you like to cold call, that's a more direct approach. Many people, however, prefer networking over cold calling, even though a lot of interviews may not turn into sales calls. To a great degree, prospecting is a mind game. If you can make prospecting an enjoyable experience, you're going to do a lot more of it. Be careful not to judge networking as too indirect. Networking continues to be a highly effective approach for many salespeople and a lot more fun than cold calling.

PART SIX

The Bigger Perspective

AFRAID OF RUNNING OUT OF REFERRALS?

The following behaviors are red flags that you have lost the *prospecting mentality*:

- You notice you have a fear of running out of referrals.

- You are protecting certain referrals or your referrals in general by not calling them.

- You notice that you are shuffling prospecting cards around daily but still not making the calls.

- You are waiting for just the right time to call.

- You find yourself thinking of reasons not to call that are not based on fact, and you have no way of proving if they are true or not. Example: "This guy lives on a nice street and has a great job. He is probably working with someone he is happy with."

- You are waiting to call on certain people until you have more experience. (This is reasonable in some cases, but usually not a good sign. Make the call; you can get help if needed.)

- You are not calling your referrals because you don't want to waste them.

- You notice that you are doing well at getting lots of referrals and then not calling them.

- You send out your referral letters and then wait so long to follow up that you are embarrassed to make the call and don't call.

- You notice that you regularly find other things to do besides call your referrals.

- You don't seem to ever have enough time to call your referrals.

- You are promising yourself on a regular basis that you will make the calls tomorrow. This reminds me of a sign I saw in front of a bar one time: FREE BEER TOMORROW.

Do you know what my advice is to people with any of the above symptoms? Take a deep breath, read through your "warm-up," and call 'em all! Just sit down and get it over with. It actually takes much more time and energy *not* to call your referrals than it does to call them. If you had a dollar for every minute you put off calling someone, how much would you have? If you spent the same amount of time calling your referrals as you did putting it off, you would make a lot more than a dollar per minute. Think about it!

I realize some people may be feeling some resistance to simply calling all your referrals. All the reasons not to make the calls are flooding into your awareness. The most important thing to realize at this point is that all those reasons are not real. They are recorded tapes in your head designed to keep you safe and away from taking any kinds of risks. You can make calls regardless of the chatter that is going on in your head. The key is to make the call. As soon as someone answers the telephone on the other end, your mind has to focus attention on talking to the other person. Your reasons not to call quickly fade into the background. The trick is to dial the telephone and let the chatter in your head just do its thing. It doesn't have to stop you. The people who become awesome at prospecting learn to take their fears and mental chatter *with* them rather than let it stop them. No matter how successful you get, there will always be a referral call that will be difficult to make at one time or another.

Call all your referrals! Intentionally run out! Guess what will happen? You will find more, I promise. Did you ever put something off and put something off, and then finally you got around to doing it and it was relatively easy? You could not figure out why you waited so long to take action. Running out of referrals is similar. Go ahead and run out. You will find more.

When you call all your referrals, a number of good things happen. You will feel proud of yourself for demonstrating that you are committed to your success by doing what you have to do. Your energy level and sense of well-being will really soar. This means you will have more energy to find more referrals. Usually people experience an increased commitment to getting referrals at this point. However, sometimes acquiring more referrals can demand that you get more creative with your methods. The following are additional ideas on how to obtain more referrals if you find yourself running low.

• Make a list of all the people you know or have ever met and ask them all if they would be comfortable introducing you to people they know. When I was in the life insurance business, I asked a friend of mine if he would help me. He said, "I believe in you but I am not very excited about life insurance. So I will introduce you to people." He introduced me to 50 — that's right 50 — of the top business and professional people in our community. I got in to see a lot of people who would otherwise have been very difficult to meet. A large number of those 50 people bought life insurance from me.

Call people you know. Take them to breakfast or to lunch. Ask them if they would be comfortable introducing you to people — not to sell them anything,

just to meet them and be a resource for the future,
and to make them smarter consumers. If they buy
something from you in the process, that's a bonus. I
have a friend in the car business who used to have a
dealership on South Logan Street in Lansing, Michigan. His radio and TV slogan was, "Get rollin' to
South Logan. If we make a buck, it's sheer luck!"
That dealership was always one of the sales leaders
in the whole country!

The moral of the story is: Go interact with people.
It's okay to enjoy the experience. A lot of people
will decide to buy from you if they like you and
your product. You don't have to feel like you need
to conquer everyone you talk to. Show them what
you've got or tell them what you do, and see if they
want to take the next step.

A word of caution: The fewer expectations you have
when you approach friends, the better. Your focus
should be on giving your friends the benefit of your
knowledge and experience, not on selling them
something. Let *them* decide what they want to do
without any pressure from you. Today more than
ever, people love to buy; they hate to be sold, especially friends. Many of your friends are going to buy
from you with this low-key approach. The hard part
is not thinking twice about the friends who don't
buy. Let them go.

• Pay attention to the names people bring up or allude
  to when you are interacting with them. You can feed
  back these names later when you ask for referrals.

• Pay attention to the kinds of activities people are
  involved in. When it comes time to ask for referrals,
  you can say: "Pete, you mentioned that you like to

play golf. Who are some of the people you know from golf?"

- The use of office directories can help your clients think of people who might be good referrals. If you are going to an office park, make a list of the people that you would like to meet from the office directory and ask your clients if they know any of them. Most likely they will. Sample language could sound something like:

You: "Joe, I plan to call on these people in your building. Do you know any of these people? Who do you like the most? Would it be okay if I said you and I have done some work together?"

- If you have some Sherlock Holmes in you, a city directory can be interesting. Before you go to your clients' house, look up the names of some of their neighbors or people who live close to them and use a similar approach.

You: "Jan, I was planning to call on _____, _____, and_____. Do you know any of these people?"

Jan: "Sure, I know them all."

You: "Who do you like the most?"

Jan: "We do things with the Joneses socially. They are great people."

You: "Would it be okay if I mentioned that we have done some work together? [Qualify as much as you like.] What does Bob do?"

If this approach makes you feel uncomfortable in any way, it probably won't work in the long run, so skip it.

THE POWER OF CONFIDENCE AND COURAGE

I have a longtime friend who has been exceptionally success-ful in the commercial real estate business. I asked him years ago how he did it. His answer really stuck with me. He said, "I am willing to jump off the cliff and learn to fly on the way down."

I had a business associate who taught me a very simple for-mula for success that has helped guide me for many years. He said, "Have a vision of what you want to accomplish, act on your intuitive instincts toward that vision, and then you trust until the last second."

What I hope you are getting from these two examples is that no matter how skilled you are, there is always an unknown el-ement. This is why confidence and courage are critical. If you are committed to asking for referrals and you find yourself not getting around to asking, you have to take some risks. You have to face your fear of the unknown elements of dealing with people. It requires some trust and faith to face the un-known. You have to believe that more of what you do is going to work than not work. Remind yourself that Babe Ruth be-came famous for hitting the most home runs, and at the same time, was the league leader in strikeouts. What would happen to your bank account if you could consistently win 51% at the blackjack table or the roulette wheel? Even though you would be losing 49% of the time, money would no longer be one of your concerns.

You have to have confidence in the value of what you do for people. You have to have confidence in the process that you take people through. You have to have confidence in your ability to help people figure out what they want and need, and then help them get it. You have to have confidence in the law of physics, which says for every action there is a reaction. The response isn't always immediate, and that is why we have to have faith. If you show you are committed to getting referrals by taking the risk of asking for them, you will get referrals.

When I speak to a group, I like to use *rolling dice* as an analogy to prospecting in general. When you roll the dice, you don't know what's going to happen. Sometimes you get winners and sometimes you get losers. You don't know whether you have a winner or a loser until you roll the dice. If you don't roll the dice, you can't win. If you don't roll the dice, you can only lose because there is only one way to roll a winner. You have to roll. It's the same with getting referrals. If you want more referrals than those that come to you, you have to ask for them. You have to face the unknown and risk asking for what you want.

My objective in writing this special report is to give you the edge you need to be able to risk asking for referrals. Hopefully this material has made you more committed to asking for referrals and brought the risk level down to a more manageable size. Be brave and remember you're looking for *chemistry and timing*. Forget about the people who don't respond positively! Armed with the proper perspective, the hunt for the right people can be great fun, and you will be paid well for your efforts. It's time to roll the dice!

WARM-UPS

One of the most important things you can do before you attempt to do any kind of prospecting is to "warm up." Just as a professional athlete would not think of going out onto the playing field without warming up, your situation is no different. The warm-up is different for prospecting. Instead of stretching your body, you *stretch your perspective*. You need to be operating from the largest perspective possible, as opposed to the narrow perspective of the analytical approach. The best way I know to do this is to read or listen to phrases that describe the larger perspective.

What follows is a series of warm-ups I have written at different times for different projects. What I recommend is that you read through all the warm-up phrases and then highlight the ones that resonate with you the most. Make a list of your favorites and add any of your own that come to mind. Reword what I have written. Make it your own. Then you can read through the list before you do any kind of prospecting or before you go on an appointment where you will ask for referrals.

Another approach that is extremely effective is to make a tape recording in your own voice of the phrases that seem to get you in the right mood. Play the tape whenever you need to get into the "prospecting mentality." Give this a try; it works!

The Referral Warm-up

Some of the warm-up phrases I have found to be the most useful for asking for referrals are:

- Referrals have been proven to be the most profitable prospecting approach for most salespeople.

- A large portion of the population is not comfortable giving referrals no matter what I do. If I get less than an enthusiastic response, I am not going to make it about me or think that I need to be different because someone else is uncomfortable giving referrals. That is their issue, not mine.

- The only way you can lose at the referral game is not to ask.

- Asking for referrals and not getting any is not losing. It is the reality of the process. Keep asking; many people are going to say yes. The key is not to make it a big deal if you ask and don't get any.

- How people respond to you when you ask for referrals is of little significance. Take whatever they say and run with it. If they are willing to help you, great. If they seem to be uncomfortable, accept their position and move on to something else.

The Prospecting Mentality

The following is the warm-up from my tape series *The Prospecting Mentality — How to Get in the Right Frame of Mind to Prospect for New Business.*

Characteristics of the Prospecting Mentality

1. Effective prospectors have an ability to continually monitor the bigger picture. They are not overly concerned with any one aspect, circumstance, or event along the path to achieving their goal. They view seeking out new business as an ever-changing flow of events rather than a predictable technical procedure. They know and accept the reality that there is always an unknown element when working with people.

2. They have a tireless ability to maintain a positive vision no matter what happens, and keep their eye on their long-term goals. Furthermore, with a positive vision and goals that feel intuitively right, they know their vision will somehow become a reality with good for all concerned.

3. They trust their ability to succeed and are not concerned with *how* they succeed, as long as it is done with integrity.

4. They trust the power of their intuitive instincts to creatively guide them along the most effective and efficient path to achieving their goals.

5. They have no fear of making mistakes since they see their mistakes as a required part of the process of reaching their goals.

6. They have no fear of failure because they view failure as merely a negative judgment about how things have turned out thus far. Their perspective says the only way to fail is to quit before it feels intuitively right to do so.

7. They do not need to know how things will turn out before taking action. They simply trust that if they do what feels right with a positive vision, they will succeed in one of two ways. They will either get the result they want or learn something that is required to achieve the result. In this way, they know in their heart and soul, they really can't lose.

8. They have fun meeting and getting to know new people. They enjoy being warm, friendly, and spontaneous with people. They have a sense of humor and a sensitivity to what others are feeling.

9. They give each call 100% of their creativity, skill and sensitivity. They treat each call as if it were a totally new experience, being ready to sense the subtle differences in people.

10. They do not care who buys and who doesn't. They are looking for the right people to work with based on the right chemistry and timing rather than trying to force a relationship with people who don't really want one.

A Prospecting Mentality "Warm-up"

1. I accept the reality of prospecting and realize that no matter how skilled I am or how wonderful my products are, some people are going to be interested and some are not.

2. I accept that I don't know which of the people I call on are going to be interested and accept the certainty that if I continue to make calls, there will be people who are interested in what I am offering. It's like rolling dice. It is guaranteed that some rolls are going to be winners. I never know for sure which ones are going to be winners until after I have rolled the dice.

3. I accept that there are plenty of people for me to work with, and if someone isn't interested in what I am offering, it may simply be that the timing isn't right for us to have a business relationship.

4. I accept the "chemistry and timing" formula that says I am going to hit it off with some of the people I meet and that some of *those* people are going to be ready for what I am offering. And for

the most part, the elements of chemistry and timing are out of my control, so I should not get overly involved in trying to make things happen that don't seem to want to happen.

5. I accept the reality that it is my responsibility to regularly initiate prospecting activity. It is as much a part of life as it is a part of my job to regularly seek out people who are interested in what I have to offer. I accept the unknown elements of prospecting and realize it is an ever-changing art rather than a predictable science. The only way I am going to know who might be interested is to make the call.

6. I accept that the only way I can lose at prospecting is not to do it. I have everything to gain with the smallest of efforts in the right direction. The key is to maintain a momentum by regularly asking people if they might have an interest in what I am offering.

A FINAL WORD

Many options have been presented in this special report. Certainly many more approaches and languages exist, and the potential combinations are endless. Any approach can work for you as long as it feels right to you. If you are not comfortable with a particular approach, forget about it. Don't even consider using it. If you like only part of an approach, only use the part that you like. The real key to being effective at asking for and getting the referrals you want is to *develop an approach that fits your values and style, an approach that feels right to you.* And remember, you are the only person in the world who knows what feels right to you.

All the knowledge in the world is useless until you put it into action. Make a commitment to yourself for at least 30 days to ask for referrals. See how you do and then recommit. By the mere fact that you have gotten this far in this text, you have demonstrated that you have the commitment you need to get the referrals you seek.

PART SEVEN
Summary

PART ONE: BENEFITS, PURPOSE & DEFINITIONS

- For most salespeople, referred leads are the most profitable source of new business. You will get in to see two to three times more people compared to cold calls, and more business will result from referrals than from any other kind of lead.

- The stronger the relationship between the referror and the person referred, the more powerful the referral.

- If you are referred, most often people will see you for a few minutes out of respect for their friend whether or not they are interested in what you have to offer.

- Rapport is a key factor in sales today. The more you have in common with someone, the more rapport you will have. When you are referred, you have a relationship in common and the likelihood that you will be favorably received is extremely high.

PART TWO: CHALLENGES AND CHANGES

- Being asked to give referrals can be very psychologically complex for the referror. Roughly speaking, about half of the people you work with are going to be comfortable giving you referrals, and *about half are not*. If you are expecting to get referrals from everyone, you are going to be disappointed.

- Asking for referrals appears to be as simple as just asking. However, the number of salespeople who experience some resistance to asking for referrals is epidemic. The main reasons for not asking for referrals fall into three categories: mechanically based conflicts, rejection-based conflicts, and approach-based conflicts. (See page 19 for detailed list.)

- If you have no psychological resistance to asking for referrals and you are not asking, it is *not* a priority. *Make it a priority.*

- Unless you are in a business where people have to come to you, you must promote yourself. Self-promotion is totally professional. If people think you are less than professional because you are asking for their help, that's their issue and something you can choose to ignore.

- If both you and your referror see you as a valued advisor who treats people with honor and respect and helps people get what *they* really want, the referror should feel that he is doing his friends a favor by introducing you.

- Call reluctance is the logical conclusion of analytical thinking in a sales environment. To effectively deal with call reluctance, you have to shift your perspective away from the narrow focus of the analytical approach. As long as you are working with a perspective that says there is a correct way to ask for referrals and if you do it just right it will work every time, you are in big trouble. The perspective required to eliminate reluctance is one that is big enough that you can see you will succeed regardless of what happens on any one call. When your perspective is big enough that it no longer matters what happens on any one call, call reluctance disappears.

- The sales approach that fits the most deeply held values of most salespeople and most prospects is one of "partnership." Being in partnership with your clients means that you help them figure out what is important to them and why it's important. When people verbalize what they want and why, this creates the motivation people need to take action. You are still there as a catalyst and to offer your expertise, but you are *on their side of the table* helping them get what they want, rather than an adversary trying to talk them into something. Taking this approach will do wonders for your effectiveness in getting referrals.

• A simple rule for getting a lot more referrals: Be someone people *want* to refer to their friends. Be the kind of person other people *want* to help.

• Saying the words exactly right is not the most important part of asking for referrals. It is *who you are being* when you ask. It is *what you feel* when you ask. It is what your clients feel as a result of what *you* are feeling when you ask for their help. Get clear about what it feels like to be who you want to be, and most any language will work.

PART THREE: BUILDING A REFERRAL TRACK

• Having a track to run on is important. Some follow it exactly, some will wing it, but you need to be clear about what you are trying to communicate.

• When is the best time to ask for referrals? Whenever the prospect or client is feeling good about you, the work you are doing, or the work you have done.

• The key elements of an effective referral track are: Get a positive affirmation. Give them a way out. Explain how the process works. Ask if they would be comfortable introducing you to people they know. Let your referror know who you are looking for. Qualify the referral.

• As you get more comfortable with asking for referrals, you will find yourself saying things you really like and that really seem to work for you. I like to call these expressions "keeper phrases." Write down your keeper phrases and review them from time to time. You don't want to hear yourself saying, "That worked so well, I stopped using it."

- Send thank-you cards to your referrors or any other gifts you feel are appropriate.

- Get permission to periodically follow up with people who have given you names to see if they have met anyone interesting.

- Find out what is working for other people. Talk to your peers and look for clues in your trade magazines.

PART FOUR: CONTACTING THE REFERRAL

- If you are sending a letter to your referrals, there are several things to include: talk benefits, give them "a way out," give them a reputation to live up to, promise to be brief, and mention your referror's name.

- Calling a referral on the telephone is like any other kind of telephone sales call. You want to be upbeat and sound like someone who is enjoying life, someone who would be interesting to meet. What you say is secondary to how you feel when you say it. If you are feeling relaxed and confident with a genuine desire to meet new people, this will come through in your voice.

- What the *Chemistry and Timing Formula* states is that if the chemistry is there in the first meeting, you continue to work with this prospect. If you determine that the chemistry is not there, you don't pursue the relationship. If the chemistry is there and the timing isn't (no current need for your product or service), put the prospect back in your tickler file for a later call.

    You are not going to be 100% accurate in your judgment of people. You will walk away from some sales you could have made with the Chemistry and Timing Formula. What salespeople typically discover is that substantial increases in income, and the sense of well-being that comes from working with people you enjoy having a relationship with, far outweigh a few missed sales from more difficult people.

PART FIVE: ALTERNATE APPROACHES

Developing Centers of Influence

- Centers of Influence can be a substantial source of referrals. The key is to find people you really connect with and who see you as a resource worthy of their business.

- Find out what your Centers are looking for and why it's important to them. Find out what you need to have to get on the short list of people they refer to. Find out how many opportunities they have to refer business to someone like yourself per year.

- Be visible to your Centers by getting your name in front of them. Be a resource by providing information and services that will help make their job easier and establish your credibility and professionalism.

The Golf Approach

- Golf is one of the most effective ways to meet people on a nonbusiness basis.

- You have a lot of time to get to know the people you are playing with, and they have a lot of time to watch how you approach the game, a reflection of how you do business.

- Invite potential clients to play but keep the conversation about business very general. Leave specifics for later. Give your guests a call in a few weeks to get together. This is a popular approach with many good golfers. Every one I have ever talked to says it's a great investment, besides being an incredible amount of fun!

The Individual Seminar Approach

• This is a half-hour presentation to one person on a topic of interest to him. This approach is especially effective for people who have extensive technical knowledge and like to teach.

• The key here is to give away some quality information and then ask your prospect for who else he knows that might appreciate this kind of information at the end of the presentation. Of course, if the chemistry and timing are there, these presentations can easily require follow-up and turn into sales.

The Networking Approach

• Most everyone today realizes the power of a network. The more people you know, the bigger your network. The bigger the network, the greater your resources.

• Networking is very social. It is not a sales interview. What you are hoping for is that the people you are talking to will ask you to get them more information on a particular product you have, or ask you how to proceed if they want to do some work with you.

• Many salespeople prefer networking over cold calling, even though many interviews will not evolve into sales calls.

PART SIX: THE BIGGER PERSPECTIVE

• If you find yourself not calling your referrals, you have likely slipped into a "low-risk mentality" that will make you fearful that you will run out of referrals. One of the best antidotes for this mindset is to call *all* your referrals. This will force you to be resourceful and figure out ways to get more referrals.

• When you call all your referrals, a number of good things will happen. You will feel proud of yourself for demonstrating that you are committed to your success by doing what you have to do. Your energy level and sense of well-being will really soar. You will have lots of energy to find more referrals.

• Creative ways to get more referrals include: making a list of everyone you know or have ever met and asking for their help, paying attention to the names people bring up or allude to during your interviews, getting the names of people you suspect your client knows from directories and then asking them if they know any of these people.

• There is no way to escape the element of the unknown when dealing with people. Confidence and courage are required to take the risks you need to take to effectively promote yourself.

• Like a professional athlete, it is good to warm up before you go into action. The difference in sales is that instead of stretching your muscles, you *stretch your perspective*. You want a perspective big enough that it doesn't matter what happens on any one call.

• The only way you can lose at the referral game —
  is not to ask.

About the Author

Sid Walker has proven to possess an exceptional aptitude for
coaching salespeople to quan-
tum leaps in both their production and the self-fulfillment they
get from their work. His expertise has evolved from over 16
years of "hands-on" experience
as a peak performance coach
working predominantly with top
sales executives in the financial
services field.

Sidney C. Walker

Sid is known for his extraordinary ability to identify the little
things that make the difference between "doing okay" and
"thriving." His specialty is helping salespeople customize their
businesses to take maximum advantage of their natural style
and strengths. The resulting increases in sales and self-esteem
are outstanding.

Prior to embarking on his peak performance coaching career,
Sid was a life insurance agent with Northwestern Mutual for
four years, specializing in Disability Income Insurance. He has
a multi-disciplinary Bachelor of Arts degree from Michigan
State University emphasizing Management and Psychology.
Sid lives in Longmont, Colorado, with his wife, Linda, and
their daughter, Tian.

Other Products by Sid Walker

Trusting Yourself
*How to Overcome the Psychological
Barriers to Reaching Your Potential
Selling Life Insurance, Investments
and Financial Planning Services.*
(book, 157 pp.)

The Prospecting Mentality
*How to Get in the Right Frame of Mind
to Prospect for New Business*
(**"The Cure for Call Reluctance"**
on four audiocassettes)

How to Double Your Sales
by Asking a Few More Questions
*Making More Sales by Helping People
Get What THEY Really Want*
(book, 126 pp.)

Two Live Recorded Coaching Sessions
*1. How to Sell Yourself with Power and Integrity
2. How to Overcome Prospecting Avoidance
and Procrastination*
(two audiocassettes)

For More Information

For information on:

- **speaking** to your group or organization
- **"in-house" workshops**
- **individual coaching** (in person or by telephone)
- **ordering** books and tapes
- *quantity discounts* on books and tapes

CALL:

High Plains Publications
800-323-6567
(24-hour answering service)